31 DAYS, 31 HORROR MOVIES
VOL. I

Bob Cram Jr

Acknowledgements

I started writing horror movie reviews on RPG.net on a whim, and the community embraced *31 Days, 31 Horror Movies* pretty much immediately. Without their interest, support and participation I don't think I would have continued writing about horror movies that month, never mind for the next 8 years! For the fourth iteration of the thread, where these reviews came from, I'd like to mention Calliope, Naxxul, Craig Oxbrow, mirober, Dweller in Darkness, Tom B, linus.larsson, Crinos, Jonas Albrecht, Patrick Y., TechnocratJT, Count_Zero, Chris Waffle King, Arizona, Brandi, Strange Visitor, Scott Dorward, evilandy, JoeNotCharles, Anaguma, malindle, jamasiel, Crothian, jimthegray, ntharotep, chiasaur11, kagechikara, AndyGuest, and molokai. You each made reading the thread just as much fun as participating in it.

My brother Scott has always shared and supported my interest in horror movies and without him I probably wouldn't have seen some of my favorites. How was *Evil Dead 2*? "It'll turn your hair white."

Bill Walker and Chris McCarthy - college roommates and fellow travellers in late-night VHS video store crawls. Our choices weren't always (or often) good, but they did usually meet our extremely basic requirements. Gore and boobs.

Pidde Andersson, reviewer extraordinaire, whose late night calls from Sweden often revolved around horror films. (I know it's not Dolph Lundgren, Pidde, you're not fooling anyone!)

My wife, Maureen Mitchell, thank you for supporting this strange interest and endeavor of mine, even if you don't always understand it.

CONTENTS

INTRODUCTION

There are actually 33 horror movie reviews in this book. And only 30 illustrations of horror movies on the cover. It's a madhouse.

I like horror movies. Hopefully you do too, or at least like reading about them, because they're the subject of this book. Shocking, I know. I used to feel like I needed to explain why I liked horror films, but I've come to realize that it's okay to just like something without needing to defend it. You're allowed to like things. Even the *Battlefield Earth* movie (you monster).

I started writing *31 Days, 31 Horror Movies* as a lark - a way to watch more horror movies and keep myself writing at the same time. The rules I set for myself were these:

- It had to be a horror movie (no sci-fi unless it crosses genres – so *Alien* works, but *Aliens* does not).
- I had to watch one a day, but I might not get to write it up for a day or two.
- No set watch-list. I'd decide that day what I'd watch. The only exception was if I got an itching for a particular film and I didn't currently have access – I'd plan around when I could rent/borrow/buy it.

I decided to do this in public, on a messageboard because... uh, I may never have had a good reason for that, actually. Maybe I'm just masochistic. It turned out to be great fun, however, and as a result I've been doing it for eight years at this point.

I have no training or education in writing reviews, so these were never intended as a truly academic exercise. I just like horror movies. I like talking about them, reading about them, writing about them and, of course, watching them. That's not to say I won't engage in any analysis or observations of theme or discussion of wider context - I will - but I'll also ramble about why watching *In Search of* led to my love of Bigfoot movies.

It's impossible for me to be objective when watching a film and so I don't even pretend to try for that in writing these reviews. In fact, I think it can be beneficial to know a reviewers background and biases when reading their take on a film, and so some of these are almost as much autobiography as they are review.

My tastes are wide, but shallow, which can be helpful if you're a horror movie fan. For you as a reader that means I'll be covering films that are critically acclaimed - like *The Exorcist* - and films that are... not so much. Like *A Cat in the Brain*. I like black and white films, exploitation films, found-footage, slasher flicks, animal attack, creature features, zombie movies, anthologies... you get the idea. If a particular review is of a genre not to your liking you can probably find something completely different a couple of pages later.

I TRY and find something to like in almost all the movies I review but the nature of the exercise - pick a movie at the last minute based mostly on fluctuations in mood, interest and availability - means that I sometimes review a movie that I end up disliking. So these aren't all recommendations, though you may find more to love in films like *Night of the Lepus* than I did.

Most of the reviews are as I originally wrote them, but there have been some edits and the occasional update or date change.

I've probably rambled on enough (or more than enough) at this point and if you've stuck with me this long - I'm sorry. There's no great punchline or denouement for this intro. I hope you enjoy the reviews. If you're a glutton for punishment you can always check out my occasional *Fear Flashback* column at ScreenageWasteland.com or maybe pick up my horror/comedy/adventure novel, *The Monster War.*

Thanks for reading!

-bob
March 30, 2019

Introduction

THE BLAIR WITCH PROJECT

"I'm so sorry..."

Directors: Daniel Myrick and Eduardo Sanchez, Producers: Robin Cowie and Gregg Hale, Written by: Daniel Myrick and Eduardo Sanchez, Starring: Heather Donahue, Michael C. Williams and Joshua Leonard

As of this writing it's been twenty years since *The Blair Witch Project* was first released. That doesn't seem possible. Twenty years? It's true, though, and we've been living with the fallout all that time.

The found footage movie wasn't invented by *TBWP* (see *Cannibal Holocaust* or maybe even *The Legend of Boggy Creek* as contenders for that title), but it certainly came into its own with *Blair Witch*'s debut. Since then we've had some good found footage movies (*[REC]*, *Paranormal Activity*), some bad (*Atrocious, The Fourth Kind*) and mostly a grab bag of mixed results (*Cloverfield, Diary of the Dead*). For years I've been expecting found footage to fade away, but with the release of films like *As Above, So Below* and *They Are Watching* it seems like it's going to be around for a long time yet.

So what about the movie that started it all? My own history with *Blair Witch* is a little complicated. I bought pretty heavily into the pre-release hype. Not in a "it's a true story!" way - though I did know people who thought that - but in a "wow, look at the way they're integrating the internet and other media into the marketing" way. It was really the first film to use what we ended up calling Viral Marketing, and they did it brilliantly. I even bought the *Blair Witch Dossier* book, which was supposed to be documents pertaining to the investigation of the filmmaker's disappearance. The book was quite fun and I was pretty primed to enjoy the movie when I finally got around to seeing it.

Unfortunately, I saw it at a second-run movie theater in Portland, Maine, and the projectionist was unaware that the movie was supposed to be shown in its original aspect ratio. Shot on 16mm and video tape the movie was filmed in 1:33:1, but the projectionist blew it wide. So I ended up watching a bunch of enormous asses walking away from me for an hour and half. It made it hard to take seriously, and I came away disappointed.

The consensus since then seems to have dismissed *The Blair Witch Project* as a mediocre film that happened to hit at the exact right time and in the exact right way. (I say that, though the movie currently has a rating of 87% on Rotten Tomatoes). I have friends who are of the opinion that it isn't even truly a horror movie, because there's nothing in it that's really scary. Certainly that's the way I came to view it - as the progenitor of a sub-genre that went on to spawn much better and more frightening films.

The thing is, I think that the pop cultural impact and time has dulled our appreciation of the actual movie. It's been copied, parodied and discussed at length. The drawbacks in filmmaking, acting, editing, pacing etc. have also been gone over again and again. It's the pieces I tend to dismiss - is the whole better than I remember?

I'm happy to say that yes, I have been unfairly maligning this film. I have not actually watched the whole thing since that initial viewing in 1999 and watching it in my dark basement with the fog pressing against the windows really made a difference in my enjoyment. The very things that I used to make fun of - bad framing, poor focus, repetitive conversations, shaky camerawork, even that up-the-nose confessional - all of that actually helps create the feeling that this is a real thing. That this could be cobbled together out of footage shot by a group of film students who were barely capable of handling their equipment. There are sections of the movie that are completely devoid of image - it's just a black frame with very, very faint noises. I found myself leaning forward at those moments, trying to make out distant sounds.

The Medium

I actually watched this on Netflix streaming. Despite owning such cinematic masterpieces as *Frogs* and *Thirteen Ghosts* I somehow never wanted to pick up a copy. It's listed as being in HD, which makes me laugh, as it's low-quality 16mm footage and videotape, but the picture was clear and the sound was good.

The Movie

The Blair Witch Project, as the opening credits announce, is presented as footage recovered after the disappearance of three young people who were filming a documentary on the Blair Witch.

There's no attempt, beyond that opening statement, to outline a story or narrative beyond that which is represented by the footage. There's no framing sequence or documentary-style interviews with family, friends and colleagues. That stuff exists - it was part of the marketing of the film - but it's not shown within the context of the film itself. I had read *The Blair Witch Dossier* before watching the film the first time and I re-read it this time to be in the same frame of mind. I think it actually enhanced the viewing process and it's recommended. It makes things creepier.

The majority of the film, after some introductory footage in and around the town of Burketsville, revolves around the three filmmakers being lost in the woods. As time goes on and they get more desperate it becomes apparent that they are being stalked by someone or something. They hear voices in the night, find weird conglomerations of sticks and piles of stones (I have one friend who can't look at rock walls without a shudder) and even endure an attack on their tent. There's no real overt violence - though there is some blood - it's just a slow-burn of creepiness that ratchets up over several days.

I've quite enjoyed some of the found footage films that have been made since 1999. [REC] is probably my favorite, but I liked *Cloverfield* and *Grave Encounters*, as examples. The thing about these movies, though, is that they're well made. Somehow the camera, shaky as it is, manages to catch exactly what's needed. It's always on when the action happens. The faces are clear and completely in-frame. The thing that I like about *Blair Witch* is that sometimes the camera is pointed at the floor. Sometimes things aren't in focus. Sometimes there's no light. Sometimes there's condensation on the lens. It's not perfect, it's so much like what it purports to be - amateur footage shot by young people with a lot of problems.

Even the acting, often derided as a very bad (I think Donahue actually won a Razzie that year), strikes me as being mostly realistic. These are people that know they're being filmed and as the movie goes along the acting actually gets better and better as they stop caring so much about how they appear on film.

It's not perfect. It drags sometimes. The acting is uneven, and Donahue in particular has a few dud moments. However, as a whole I think it's extremely effective. By the time we reached the end sequence and the house I'd bought into their tension so completely that I had to refrain from yelling at the screen, "don't go in the basement! What the hell is wrong with you!"

The Bottom Line

I'm glad I made myself take another look at this film. It's a lot better than I remember it being and there are things that it does that no other found footage film has done as well since. It feels real, which is the point of these things, and all the amateurishness actually enhances that feeling. If you haven't seen *The Blair Witch Project* in a while it might be worth a repeat viewing.

SHIVERS (AKA THEY CAME FROM WITHIN)

"Roger, I had a very disturbing dream last night."

Director: David Cronenberg, Producer: Ivan Reitman, Written by: David
Cronenberg, Starring: Paul Hampton, Lynn Lowry, Barbara Steele

Shivers is a movie about a sex zombie apocalypse.

It's also a movie about the isolation of modern life, relationships, infidelity, body horror, mad science, and venereal diseases. In other words, It's a David Cronenberg film.

For the longest time *Shivers* was the one early Cronenberg film I hadn't seen (the feature releases, that is - I still haven't seen *Stereo* or *Crimes of the Future*). I'd heard about it, but could never find a copy. I remember reading an article about it during the 1980s - probably around the time that *The Fly* was being released - that called it the goriest and most disturbing of his films. By that point we'd had *Rabid*, *The Brood*, *Scanners*, and *Videodrome*, so that was saying something.

So it was always on my 'must watch' list, but I never was able to come across a copy - VHS or DVD. It's been on my Netflix "Availability Unknown" list for years and I'd given up on ever seeing it.

Forward to yesterday. I'd been planning on watching a Cronenberg film anyway - I picked up a copy of the Criterion Collection release of *Scanners* last month specifically for *31 Days*. I'll end up watching it this month sometime, but during the day I got a notification from Netflix saying that *Shivers* was now available on streaming. Plans went out the window - I was finally going to see one of the great white whales of my horror movie list.

The Medium

I'm guessing that someone is re-releasing *Shivers* on Blu-ray, because the streaming version is pretty high quality. Actually, let's not guess, the Internet is our friend... Yeah, looks like Arrow is releasing a Blu-ray edition. Region B only, though, so I won't be able to pick up a copy until a US company releases it - I'm not holding my breath.

The picture quality, as mentioned, is pretty darn good for a streaming movie made for a shoestring in 1975. There were a few low-quality shots with some noise, but that could easily have been my connection. This is probably as good as it's gonna get for us in Region A. Enjoy your Region B release, Greenland.

The Movie

Shivers starts off with a come-on, one of those real estate video advertisements. This one is advertising the latest in luxury, the Starliner apartment complex. The building sits on an island reachable only be a single bridge. It's a self-contained living area with all the amenities one could want - including a store, a medical clinic, heated swimming pool, and parking garage. This is the primary movie location, of course. A modern, swinging apartment building - with plenty of great suites still available.

There's something a little sterile about the Starliner, though. It's a bit too shiny and clean. It's just like the brochure - a little lifeless. Of course that's all on the surface. Dig a little deeper and you'll find all kinds of things going on - horrible things.

Cronenberg introduces us to the location via a young couple who are inquiring about an apartment. They're buying into the illusion. Meanwhile, he juxtaposes their scenes with a brutal sequence going on in one of those very apartments. An older man is struggling violently with a very young woman. As the couple downstairs peruse listings and listen to the salesman's patter the young woman upstairs is strangled, stripped, cut open, and has acid poured into the incision. The older man then promptly cuts his own throat.

This is pretty messed up stuff. The actress playing the victim is young enough that it almost felt like it was crossing a line. In that respect the movie immediately feels a little dangerous, a little transgressive. What sorts of things will a director do who's willing to do that?

Worse things, actually. Much worse things.

The older man turns out to be a scientist named Hobbs. The doctor-in-residence at Starliner - Roger St. Luc - is brought in during the police investigation and soon learns that Hobbs had a grant that involved using parasites as organ replacement. He begins to suspect that Hobbs may have been conducting his experiments in the field.

Meanwhile, a man named Nick is obviously sick, having developed some strange lumps on his stomach. He won't go see the doctor, but his wife goes to Dr. St. Luc anyway, and convinces the doctor to come up to their apartment later to see her husband. Unfortunately, things are going from bad to worse with Nick, and he ends up vomiting blood into the tub. A slimy trail leading down the drain reveals that more has come out of him than just blood.

St. Luc learns that the murdered woman was, despite her schoolgirl appearance, very promiscuous and has slept with a number of the men in the complex - including Nick. All of the men are now developing weird cysts in their stomachs. An associate of Hobbs tells St. Luc that the parasite is transmitted like a venereal disease and that it acts like an aphrodisiac. It makes people amorous so it can spread.

And spread it does. The gross, sluglike things are moving all around the complex. They leap through the air to latch on to people's faces, they burst from stomachs and crawl out of mouths. In a memorable sequence one of the parasites exits a bathtub drain and slides between a woman's legs.

Things begin to spin out of control and the inhabitants quickly degenerate into wandering mobs of crazed rapists. In one of the most disturbing scenes an infected man enters an elevator with a woman and her young girl. The doors close. Later, the blood soaked little girl passes on the infection.

I told you. Much worse things.

The ending falls down a little bit, as the action devolves to a standard set of zombie movie chase scenes. The doctor tries to escape with his lover/nurse and they're both hunted throughout the complex before a final apocalyptic orgy at the heated pool. There's a nicely creepy denouement the next day with various people - who we know to be infected - leaving the apartment complex by car, one by one, heading to the city to spread the parasite. Our 'hero' included.

Technically, there are issues. The lighting is pretty flat, as it is in a lot of low-budget 1970's films. The editing is uninspired, as is the framing (with a few exceptions). The effects range from fairly realistic to laughably bad (it's really hard to make a penis-shaped slug seem threatening when it moves). Action sequences - of which there are too many as the film progresses - are poorly choreographed. The behavior of the parasites is inconsistent, as if Cronenberg changed his mind several times over the course of the film.

The Bottom Line

I had ups and downs while watching *Shivers*. It's uneven and frustrating at times. People act in unbelievable ways. Some of the dialogue - particularly from the lead male - is recorded so low as to be almost inaudible. Some of the effects are bad enough that they puncture any tension a scene has built up.

And yet - I kept thinking about it after the credits rolled. The obvious references to STDs are only one layer of a complex film. There's a level that's a commentary on how, in a modern society, we never really know our neighbors and what's going on behind closed doors. There's a condemnation and fear of science run amok. There are questions of sexual identity and sexual politics. There's fear and repulsion at our own fleshy nature.

I think, in the end, the film works despite itself. It's rough in spots - and sometimes seems to be working primarily as a low-budget exploitation film - but it's an intriguing filmmaker's first foray into questions he'd explore in much more accomplished ways in films like *Rabid* and *The Fly*.

THE FLY (1958)

"Help meeee!"

Director: Kurt Neumann, Producer: Kurt Neumann, Written by: James Clavell, Starring: Al Hedison, Patricia Owens, Vincent Price

I've long labored under a misconception about the 1958 version of *The Fly*, one only made clear to me today. For some reason I've always thought that this movie is a sequel to an older film, a black and white movie featuring a creature that has a much larger head. However, when I went looking for the 'original' I was astonished to discover that the black and white movie I remember is actually the sequel! Despite the fact that the original was shot in color the sequel - *The Return of the Fly* - was shot in black and white (though still in Cinemascope, which is a little weird). I'm assuming that was for budgetary reasons. I must have seen the sequel first and simply assumed it was the original film.

I'm sure I saw both of them at my grandmother's house, probably on a rainy Saturday afternoon. It seems like I saw most of the 1950's creature features sitting on that couch, a plateful of cookies or (if I was lucky) coffee squares in front of me. I don't know which channel it was that was constantly running old sci-fi and horror movies, but I'm not sure my childhood would have been the same without it.

It's actually been a long time since I've watch this version of *The Fly*. The only thing I remembered clearly about this version was the horrific spiderweb scene, though I'd actually gotten the actors mixed up and in my memory it was Vincent Price struggling in the web. I was already arachnophobic, so that penultimate scene burned itself in my mind.

I will, occasionally, when I need something, imitate the sound of the struggling 'white headed' fly - "help meeeee, help meeeee!" My wife will look at me with a mixture of pity and... well, let's be fair, it's mostly pity.

The Medium

I watched this on Netflix streaming and, as has been the case with much of my recent streaming viewing, the quality was quite good. Not Blu-ray level, but satisfying even on my larger TV. Having now seen it, I'll probably be looking out for the Blu-ray release, if only for the commentary.

The Movie

The Fly is a bit strange for a horror movie. It's structure is different from most monster movies, in that the monster doesn't even make its first appearance until 2/3 of the way through the film. Rather than give us a shock or two up front to keep our interest the movie unfolds slowly and methodically.

In some ways it's more a mystery than a horror movie. It starts off with the apparent murder of a scientist, Andre Delambre, by his wife, Helene. It's a horrific death - crushed in an industrial press - but it's 1958 and the gore is suggested rather than explicit. Much of the first half hour of the film is spent trying to figure out why Helene would have done such a thing. They were a seemingly happy couple in the Ward and June Cleaver mold, but with lots of money. She freely admits to the murder, but refuses to say why. In general, she seems very self-possessed and clear-headed - except when it comes to flies. She has an unnatural focus and hysteria around one fly in particular - a fly with a white head.

Her brother-in-law Francois (a restrained Vincent Price) and the police inspector attempt to figure things out. Francois lies to Helene and tells her that he has the fly, but will let it go unless she tells him the truth. At that point the real story begins to unfold in flashback, as Helene tells the story of what led to that night and the industrial press.

It's the standard 'man meddling in things he was never meant to know' storyline at that point, with Andre discovering teleportation and trying to work out the kinks. Helene even has a monologue about how fast technology is moving and how it's leaving morality behind. Things start to go wrong when Andre tests the machinery on the family cat and the cat never arrives. There is an eerie, disembodied howl for a few moments afterward, which was a nice - if rare at that point - creepy bit.

Of course things go horribly wrong and when Andre tries to teleport himself a fly ends up in the chamber at the same time. Their genetic material is mixed and Andre ends up with a fly head and arm, while the fly ends up with the same parts of Andre. We don't see this occur - actually, even after we know something has gone wrong we still don't see the monster for another fifteen or twenty minutes. Andre keeps his head covered and his arm hidden in his jacket. This actually works quite well - as a viewer I was just as horrifically fascinated as Helene.

The effects when Andre's head and arm are revealed are pretty good, much better than I expected and/or remembered. The fly head is much sleeker and the mouth parts more animated than in the sequel - it looks weirdly believable. The actor - the same who played the normal Andre - does an excellent job while unable to speak or even use facial expressions.

By the time we see the monster the movie is almost over. A hunt for the 'white headed' fly in an effort to reverse the process goes awry and it escapes. Faced with a failing intellect and struggle to control his own body, Andre opts for death and enlists Helene to help him - but not before destroying his lab equipment and notes.

The most horrific sequence - the finding of the fly with the head and arm of Andre, being consumed by a spider - comes mere minutes from the end. It leaves a lasting impression and is pretty damn awful even now.

The cinematography is excellent, with the wide CinemaScope presentation and lush color giving the whole film a feeling of quality you don't expect from your average creature feature. The acting is also excellent for the time and Vincent Price is more restrained and thoughtful than in some of his later pictures. Patricia Owens as Helene is the real star, though, doing an excellent job with what is often a thankless role. When she wasn't forced to be the doting housewife she comes across as very strong and capable - someone willing to do whatever it takes to protect her family. She moves easily between hysteria and steely determination.

I didn't really notice the music, which is a rarity for 1950's monster movies - I expect to find the horn section blaring a five note monster theme at every opportunity.

The pacing is, as already mentioned earlier, quite measured. The movie is very much a slow burn and there was a feeling on my part that the filmmakers might have been a little embarrassed to be making a horror movie. The thing is, it really works - you know something horrible has happened - something awful enough to make a doting wife kill her beloved husband. It's the reveal that's the thing, and even knowing what was coming I still bought in.

The Bottom Line

I'd forgotten how good this movie was. *The Fly* is very much a 1950's horror movie, but the production values and general quality are a level or two above that of most monster pictures of the time. Yes, it's a little slow - but the payoff is worth it.

OCULUS

"Hello again. You must be hungry."

Director: Mike Flanagan, Producers: Marc D. Evans, Trevor Macy, Jason Blum, Written by: Mike Flanagan, Jeff Howard, Starring: Karen Gillan, Brenton Thwaites, Katee Sackhoff

I'm little pissed at *Oculus*.

Look, I'm okay with the bad guy winning, I really am. In fact, I kind of dig those movies where the assumptions that the protagonists are going to win are upended. I'm okay if the vampire outsmarts the heroes or whatever - especially if she's hundreds of years old (like the mirror in *Oculus*). However, there needs to be a chance - no matter how long the odds. So the ending of *Oculus* by itself doesn't bother me.

What bothers me is that at a certain point I realized that it didn't matter what Kaylie and Tim did, they were screwed. From that moment on there was really no tension for me. If it had happened right at the end, that might be okay - in fact it probably would be awesome, because the Oculus would have tricked me as well. Unfortunately there was still plenty of movie to go when I came to that realization.

And it's too damn bad, because there was a lot of good tension and scares and even horror until that moment, (It's the iPhone/fiancé sequence, if you're wondering).

The Medium

DVD from Netflix. Yeah, they still do those. Looked fine, no extras.

The Movie

It's a good setup. A young man, Tim, is being released from a mental institution at the age of 21. He's been in there since the age of 11 for killing his father (who had killed his mother). He's met by his sister Kaylie who reminds him of a promise they made that night - that promise being to kill the mirror that they blame for driving both parents insane.

The mirror, it transpires, manipulates your perceptions, makes you see things that are so realistic that you might even take a bite out of a light bulb, thinking it was an apple. The sister has made preparations to document the phenomena in order to exonerate her brother before they destroy the mirror. She's had the mirror brought to the old house and set up a bunch of equipment to both document things and provide a number of safeguards. The brother - having had ten years of therapy - no longer believes the mirror had anything to do with it, and Kaylie needs to convince him as well.

So much misery could have been avoided if someone had just dropped the damn thing one of the several times it gets moved.

Anyway, not a bad setup for a horror film. Lots of disturbing imagery and the first sequence where the two kids do something on tape that they don't remember doing in reality is a pretty good one.

Part of the film takes place in flashback, revealing the events leading up to the night the parents died. These sections start out as pretty obvious flashbacks, but during the course of the film they start becoming part of the phenomena as the characters and the film transition between the two time periods. It's a subtle shift and a nice way of blurring reality for both the characters and the audience.

The actors do an excellent job and Katee Sackoff as the mother is great as she slowly descends into paranoia and violence. The girl who plays the young Kaylie is also fantastic and is probably someone to watch in the future. Everyone else - including Amy Pond - is really good except for the actor playing the young Tim. He's not bad, but he's awkward in a way that a lot of child actors are. I probably wouldn't have noticed if the actress playing the sister hadn't been so damn good.

The tension ratchets up considerably as things go along and you begin to question everything the character see, hear and do. At points it feels like the past is actively stalking them through the house. It feels like things are going bad, but there's still that crack in the mirror - evidence that there's a way to hurt it. (That the flashbacks show there is no crack means we know that it's something that happened during that horrible night.)

And then... and then you realize that the monster is not only not playing fair, that it's pretty much omnipotent. That nothing the characters do matter, because there's really no chance for them to know what they're seeing/doing. The movie tries to paper over this early on by intimating that technology will show what really is happening. However, during the scene with the iPhone and the fiancé that's revealed to be useless as well. I mean - you're viewing the technology through compromised eyes. It doesn't really matter what the screen is showing.

After that, it all feels inevitable. There's no suspense, no real story left. You know how it's going to end. It left me feeling deflated and annoyed.

The Bottom Line

So close. *Oculus* is not a bad movie, really - and for other people it's possible (or even probable) that the thing that bothered me won't bother them at all. For me it really undercut a strong showing, and I'm ticked at the loss of opportunity more than anything.

I also found myself thinking that this might have worked better as two separate films. Make the flashbacks a movie by itself - giving more time to the parents and the dissolution of the family - and then a sequel that's the modern day. That they defeated it (sorta) once would make me more willing to buy into that chance the second time around.

BIGFOOT DOUBLE FEATURE!

The 1970's were a really weird time in general, and Bigfoot seemed a part of that. He was everywhere on TV - a segment of *In Search Of* was devoted to him, there was a kids show called *Bigfoot and Wildboy*. He was even on *The Six Million Dollar Man* (where he was actually a robot from outer space)!

Multiple movies also explored the Bigfoot legend and associated "ape men" stories from around the country. *The Legend of Boggy Creek* is probably the most famous of these, though you could make a case for that title going to *Shriek of the Mutilated* instead. Certainly the docu-drama format *Boggy Creek* pioneered was the inspiration for the two movies I watched for this theme weekend.

SASQUATCH, THE LEGEND OF BIGFOOT
"To this day, that canyon is called Ape Canyon."

Director: Ed Ragozzino, Producers: Ronald D. Olson, John Fabian, Written by: Ed Hawkins, Ronald D. Olson, Starring: George Lauris, Steve Boergadine, Jim Bradford, Ken Kenzle

This movie scared the poop out of me when I was a kid. Even now the Ape Canyon story and the ululating wail of the creature still cause a shiver.

Sasquatch, TLoB was the only one of the Bigfoot movies that I can remember seeing as a kid. I'm not sure where or when that was - I almost think it must have been on HBO. Regardless, it made an impression.

The Medium

I watched this streaming on Amazon, mostly because I'd heard it was - if not exactly 'restored' - cleaned up and of a higher quality than you'd get on YouTube. I'm not sure if that's true, though, as it's a pretty poor quality video. That may just be down to source material, as it appears to be shot on 16mm (and in spots seems to have been shot on Super8 instead).

The Movie

Sasquatch ostensibly follows an expedition into the wilderness of British Columbia on a mission to track, capture and tag a Bigfoot. It's a long expedition and they bring along quite the cast of notable 70's characters, including The Skeptical Newsman, the Indian Tracker, the Wise Old Mountain Man and the Comic Relief Cook. All these roles are written and portrayed pretty large, but they're not completely awful.

The opening sequence sets the tone as we're shown a lot of footage of various animals in their natural setting. Then the music gets menacing and we're treated to some POV shots of... something. Something big moving through the forest. The animals are startled and flee before we finally see the shadow of a man-like thing at the edge of a mountain pond.

That's actually the whole movie in a nutshell. Lots of nature shots followed by some vaguely menacing music and a sketchy look at the title monster.

For what it is - that being a 1970's low budget creature-feature disguised as a nature docu-drama - it's fairly effective. There are way too many nature shots and some obviously staged animal attacks, but there's also some good character moments, some creepy photography and one good musical cue. The monster itself is barely glimpsed, even in the final attack on the expedition camp. That's for the best, as it works quite well in tiny doses, but I get the impression it would not do so well in the full light of day.

The best parts of the movie are the two stories told about Bigfoot attacks in the past. There's a decent one about two trappers at a distant pond where only one of them makes it out alive. The one about the Ape Canyon attack is the one that sticks in the mind, however. It's told by the Wise Old Mountain Man and relates the story of an attack on some miners in the area of Mt. St. Helens. It's portrayed in pretty tame terms, but it really left an impression on the young me and has some good jump scares. The wail of the Bigfoot is really showcased here and is pretty effective, even now.

The movie culminates in a remote valley where the crew sets up a technological barrier to track the Bigfoot. Things go awry, of course, and the camp is assaulted by multiple creatures. It's frenetic and pretty dark, but effective.

The Bottom Line

Well, *Sasquatch, The Legend of Bigfoot* is not quite as scary as I remember. It's not even really that good a movie - I don't think there IS a really good Bigfoot movie (let me know if you've seen something you think qualifies). That being said, there's still some fun to be had with the cheesiness of it all and the stories aren't bad.

And that wail. Gah.

THE LEGEND OF BIGFOOT
"Whatta bunch of hogwash!"

Director: Harry Winer, Producers: Stephen Houston Smith, Ivan Marx, Don Reese, Written by: Paul Labrot, Harry Winer, Starring: Ivan Marx, Peggy Marx

This is another Bigfoot docudrama and in the big picture it's very similar to the earlier film. However, it's immensely boring and there's no tension to be had at all. And the voice over guy sounds like the animated DNA strand in *Jurassic Park*. I'd seen it once before, but it's been a long time and I thought, "it can't be as boring as I remember it being."

Well, yeah, it can.

The Medium

I saw this via Archive.org. The quality is atrocious, but about the same as YouTube. I've never seen this one for sale in DVD format, actually.

The Movie

The Legend of Bigfoot is a bunch of footage shot by a guy named Ivan Marx. He purports to be an animal tracker and filmmaker and is also the narrator. The film is supposedly a culmination of his 10 years of research into Bigfoot.

There is a lot of nature footage. I mean A LOT. It's 95% of the film. Marx tries to connect Bigfoot to various blurry and dark shots of the woods, but there's not a lot of it. There ARE several shots of

Bigfoot, but they're even less convincing than in *Sasquatch, TLoB* - and they're supposed to be actual footage! (That is always, somehow, far less clear and in focus than every other wildlife shot the guy takes.)

After the obligatory "I was a skeptic too" moments the narrator formulates a theory of Bigfoot migration by staring at a map full of dots (at least he didn't put a ruler on the map and connect them). He decides to follow the dots north and try and prove his theory.

After a long, boring trip in which the biggest piece of excitement is a sequence with glowing dots in the distance (supposedly Bigfoot's eyes - it looks like muppet, or maybe a distant car) Marx returns to a place near his house and proceeds to photograph some Bigfoots. Bigfeet? More than one Bigfoot, anyway. There's some moralizing about them being part of nature. I dunno - at a certain point I really stopped paying attention to the guy (especially when he'd grouse about all those 'scientists' and the people 'making money off my footage').

The Bottom Line

The Legend of Bigfoot is a terrible, slow, boring movie. Some of the wildlife photography might have been good for its time, but it's all blurry and faded now. Good if you need something to fall asleep to.

THE TUNNEL (2011)

Director: Carlo Ledesma, Producers: Andrew Denton, Julian Harvey, Enzo Tedeschi, Anita Jacoby, Valeria Petrenko, Ahmed Salama, Peter Thompson, Written by: Julian Harvey, Enzo Tedeschi, Starring: Bel Deliá, Andy Rodoreda, Steve Davis, Luke Arnold

I've had a mixed reaction to Australian found footage horror films. I really did not like *Uninhabited*, which felt poorly produced, written, and acted, despite some glorious scenery. *Lake Mungo* on the other hand - though perhaps not strictly a found footage movie - is a movie I consider an underappreciated gem.

So I approached *The Tunnel* with a bit of trepidation, despite having had it recommended by a few folks whose opinion on horror movies I respect. I'm happy to say that it comes down closer to the *Lake Mungo* side of things, though it doesn't quite reach the same level.

The Medium

The Tunnel was a crowd-funded production and was initially released via BitTorrent for free, though it can now be purchased on streaming platforms and on DVD. I tried watching the film via one of the YouTube releases, but the quality of these is uniformly poor. For a found footage film, that's a killer. Though you can download a high-res version from any number of torrent sites legally, I decided to rent it via Amazon. While the picture was not high-definition it was considerably better than the YouTube versions.

The Movie

The Tunnel follows a news crew as they investigate why government authorities have suddenly abandoned a plan to recycle millions of gallons of water that have filled several abandoned tunnels beneath the city of Sydney. Man that's a mouthful. There's a drought, government representatives announce a plan to recycle water found in underground tunnels. After an election, that plan is abandoned with no reason given.

Natasha, a journalist, decides to investigate. She and her crew - cameraman Steven, sound guy Tangles, and producer Peter - are unable to get anyone in the government to talk, so they descend into the tunnels to try and uncover the truth.

Things go well, and they all return alive.

Okay, no, that's not at all what happens. Instead, they find evidence that the tunnels were recently inhabited by the homeless, but they've all disappeared. Then, while filming a sequence involving an old emergency bell, Tangles disappears. In the frantic search for him the others find a room with blood splattered on the walls and Tangles' bloody flashlight. Worse, they realize that a hand-held camera - the only one with night vision - has been moved. Reviewing the footage reveals that someone or something has been watching them.

Things go quickly downhill from there, with a horrific something stalking them through the tunnels. Obligatory dodgy camera lights and things seen only briefly in the night vision camera are the order of the day. The maps are not quite right, the batteries are not all charged and personal tensions endanger everyone. Not all of them will live to see the light of day again.

There's nothing really new going on here - we've seen a lot of this in previous found footage movies. However, that's nothing against the film. They make great use of what they have - in particular a really atmospheric underground setting. The footage from the cameras is treated with more thoughtfulness than you might expect, giving decent excuses for the variation in film quality. The stuff shot in the color camera by the professional is, for course, framed and shot better than the video from the handheld, which is held by non-technical crew and often out of focus or aimed at the ground/bodypart/wall. Using both cameras allows the filmmakers to have their cake and eat it too, in that they get some scenes that are nicely shot and others that have all of that shakey, amateur look that's bread and butter for the found footage genre, and it makes a consistent sort of sense.

The location is the real star of the film. The tunnels and abandoned rooms that are the background for events are great - full of creepy atmosphere. They did some fun stuff with look-alike corridors in that at a couple of points I thought - as did the characters - that they were heading down a series of hallways that we'd already seen, but instead ran into a dead end or a different room.

The monster isn't half-bad either, and used sparingly. It's almost never (if at all) shot with the color camera and we're reduced to picking out details in a blur of movement or extreme darkness.

The acting ranges from above average to mediocre, with the main female lead falling into the latter category, unfortunately. She's got a pretty flat affect and I'm not sure whether that's the character or the actress. I could have done without her being portrayed as a control freak more concerned with her career than her crew - that was already annoying when it was used in *The Blair Witch Project*.

The main drawbacks to the film are the interviews. The movie is set up - not unlike *Lake Mungo* - as a documentary using interviews with the survivors and the footage that they brought back. These don't do the movie any favors and serve mostly to tell us who is going to live, who is going to die and to kill any suspense or momentum built up in the found footage parts.

The Bottom Line

The Tunnel doesn't really tread any new territory, but it's an effective found footage film nonetheless, especially given its budget constraints. It makes great use of the medium and of its locations to create more mood than terror - though there are some good jump scares to be had.

I do think the movie would be better served by removing the interview sections and simply presenting the found footage parts as-is. I think it would move quicker, build more consistently and wouldn't give us time to ponder the dodgier aspects of the production.

LIFEFORCE

"That girl was no girl."

Director: Tobe Hooper, Producers: Yoram Globus, Menahem Golan, Written by: Dan O'Bannon, Don Jakoby, Starring: Steve Railsback, Peter Firth, Frank Finlay, Mathilda May

Lifeforce is a weird movie. It's an exploitation film presented in Hammer sci-fi terms on a 1980's blockbuster budget. *The Vampire Lovers* as imagined by Nigel Kneale. There are special effects by a *Star Wars* veteran, a bombastic score by the composer who created the *Pink Panther* theme, a script by the guy who wrote *Alien*, and it's directed by the man who gave us *The Texas Chainsaw Massacre*.

I'm not going to pretend that I first saw this movie for the special effects or because I liked the director. In 1986 the only reason to see this movie - which bombed at the box office in 1985 - was because of Mathilda May. Yeah, there was that awesome *Fangoria* cover featuring one of the desiccated zombies, but I'm sure it was the breathless assertion "she's naked for the whole movie!" that suckered me in.

I remember being a bit disappointed. Not in May, as she was exactly as advertised, but in the movie as a whole. There was something there, some bigger movie that seemed to be weirdly truncated. The effects weren't quite as realistic as *Fangoria* had made them appear and the story seemed disjointed and a little herky-jerky, as if the director couldn't quite decide on the pace. I wrote it off as a B picture that had somehow gotten an A budget and whose main claim to fame would forever be the breasts of its star.

Fast forward several years and I'm re-evaluating a bunch of horror movies I had written off in my youth. This had all been precipitated by a viewing of *Halloween* - a movie I had discarded as being all reputation with no real skill or scares. I'd watched it again and had been astonished at the difference between my memory and the actual film - how good it really was. So I was picking up other films that I'd dismissed and *Lifeforce* was one of them.

While not experiencing exactly the same level of revelation as with *Halloween*, it IS a much better film than I remembered it being. Ms. May is in no way diminished by this re-evaluation.

The Medium

I found a used copy of the Scream Factory Blu-ray release of *Lifeforce*. This is certainly the best the film has ever looked, with a clean and crisp presentation and, notably, much richer color. There are a fair amount of extras, including two audio tracks, a making of featurette, cast interviews and both the extended and theatrical release.

The Movie

Lifeforce is based on a book called *Space Vampires* by the prolific Colin Wilson. I recently saw a copy of that book at a local flea market and wish I'd known then, as I would have picked it up. The title was changed to try and appeal to a wider mainstream audience, but the original title really tells you all you need to know. There are vampires. They're from outer space.

An expedition to Halley's Comet finds an ancient spacecraft hidden within the corona. Upon investigation they find thousands of desiccated corpses of a bat-like creature - and three perfectly preserved humanoids encased in crystal. They decide to take the three humanoids back to Earth (as well as one of the bat things).

Much of this sequence was cut in the US, and I'm not sure why. It's got some decent special effects and the alien ship is appropriately creepy. It helps set the mood and tone of the picture and I think having it removed did the film a disservice. It does make the movie seem more like a straightforward sci-fi film at first, but I think having it restored improves the story immensely.

Thirty days later the Earth spaceship enters an Earth orbit, but ground control (the British Space Agency - which seems like a *Quatermass* reference) can't establish communications. A rescue mission finds the ship gutted by a fire, its crew all dead, except for the commander, Carlsen, who is missing. They also find the unharmed bodies of the three humanoid aliens.

The bodies are taken back to Earth where a team of scientists are put to work trying to figure out what they are, but one - the female of the group - awakens and sucks the life out of a hapless security guard. Despite being in a facility full of security guards (and apparently also full of of glass-walled rooms) the girl escapes.

These sequences are pretty effective. Yes, the woman is naked the whole time. Yes, this is pretty distracting. However this is actually part of the point - the security guards don't take a pretty, naked woman seriously and get shocked into unconsciousness for their presumption. Though she's naked there's little actually sexual about her behavior - even when she's kissing the guard or telling one of the scientists to 'use' her body, she's slightly distant. And always predatory.

In fact there are a lot of sexual situations that don't feel very sexual in this movie. Carlsen - having escaped the fire - turns out to have a connection with the female vampire and has several intimate encounters with her that all feel tentative and cold. There's more heat in a scene with a male victim coming to life and draining the doctor that was about to cut him open. I can't help but feel like this distance is due to a certain discomfort on the part of the director. I think this would have been a very different film if it had been directed by, say, David Cronenberg.

Things unspool pretty quickly from the woman's escape on. She jumps bodies, sending Carlsen and a member of the SAS on a chase around England trying to find her before she drains/infects too many people. The male vampires awaken and spread the infection. One of the scientists discovers a way to kill them - stabbing them through the 'energy center' of their body with iron - but too late to do him much good. Patrick Stewart (in wheelchair, no less) makes an appearance as a man possessed by the female vampire (I'm fairly sure the kiss that he and Steve Railsback's Carlsen share is also restored. I don't remember it from the US release).

The final act of the film finds London under attack by the vampire plague with the ship - now free of the comet and hovering over London - sucking up the souls, the 'lifeforce' of the victims, like some giant spooky Hoover vacuum of doom. Carlsen heads into the city for a final confrontation with the woman leading to a semi-spectacular conclusion featuring nakedness, glowing clouds and a huge sword.

Watching the movie this time around I can see why I was disappointed originally. I was expecting a completely different kind of movie. I'd seen *Poltergeist* and heard about *The Texas Chainsaw Massacre,* so I went in thinking I would see something gory and horrifying with a Stephen Spielberg level of production quality. Needless to say, that's not quite what you get in *Lifeforce*.

Instead you get a much... smaller feeling movie. More intimate, I guess. The setting and scale of production doesn't ever reach quite far enough for the epic story. Even the climactic, apocalyptic end sequences in a London full of zombie-like vampires feels like it was shot on a set - which it probably was. What it ends up feeling like is a Hammer production from an earlier time - like a lost *Quatermass* film. Its largely British cast and English locations enhance this impression.

The special effects are mostly decent, though they remind you that glowing blue clouds were the pinnacle of awesome in the 1980's. The zombies are a little too static and puppet-like for me now, but there's still some fun to be had in various sequences, particularly a scene in which a caged zombie runs at the bars of his cage only to explode into dust. The more sci-fi sequences are quite good and make a welcome addition.

The much ballyhooed nudity is still a distraction, but less of one than I remember. The film shies away from more complicated questions of sexuality and gender identity, despite plenty of opportunities to explore them in more depth. Again, I wonder how that would have been handled by a more daring director. Problematically, the naked males are treated very differently than the female - and are never presented completely naked. A scene in which Carlson slaps and struggles with a woman who has been recently possessed by the female alien is also difficult to watch, and a throwaway line to the effect of the woman being a masochist does little to reduce the discomfort. (Though another line - "She wants me to hurt her!" has the possibility of more depth, as you're not sure whether he's referring to the actual woman or the vampire.)

The Bottom Line

Watching *Lifeforce* as if it was a Hammer picture really enhances the experience for me. Not being fifteen anymore also lets me appreciate the acting on a different level, particularly the way Matilda May controls and overpowers every scene she's in, regardless of her supposed vulnerable state.

It's still a flawed movie, but it's much better than I remember it being, and is often quite fun and interesting in weird ways. There's a really good exploitation horror flick hiding in here. Or a fairly decent *Quatermass* film. They just don't quite gel together.

ZOMBIE (AKA ZOMBI 2, AKA ZOMBIE FLESH EATERS)

"There was a man down there."

Director: Lucio Fulci, Producers: Ugo Tucci, Fabrizio De Angelis, Written by: Elisa Briganti, Dardano Sacchetti, Starring: Tisa Farrow, Ian McCulloch, Richard Johnson, Al Cliver

It's not October if I don't watch a Lucio Fulci movie.

I love Italian zombie movies. They're almost all terrible, with incomprehensible plots, incredibly bad dubbing, over-the-top gore that is also really fake looking, and more casual rape/misogyny/nudity than you can shake a stick at. And yet, they tickle me. As I've said before, I can almost always find something to enjoy in them - even *Burial Ground*. (Though what it was I enjoyed in that movie escapes me at the moment...)

Zombie, or *Zombi 2* as it was released in Italy (to take advantage of the popularity of *Dawn of the Dead*, which was released as *Zombi* in Italy), is the king of them all. It's the template on which they're all based and is - in energy, creativity, technical skill and complete over-the-top gonzo-ness - the best of them. Does that mean it's a good movie? Well, I guess it depends on what you're looking for. A plot that holds together, realistic characterizations, good acting? You're out of luck. Inventive makeup effects, shocking thrills, an atmospheric location? Now we're getting somewhere.

I came to *Zombie* pretty late in my horror viewing. I distinctly remember that I was browsing the horror stacks at a local music/ video store and coming up empty. It was late in the day and I was looking for something - anything - that would scratch that itch for a new horror movie. I think this was in the 90's, a decade that was a little rough on horror fans. Down in the corner of the last row I saw a black-case DVD with an awesome looking zombie on the cover. Dude - there are WORMS in the guy's EYE! And the tagline - 'We are going to eat you' - that's pure gold. This was the Anchor Bay release, which I still have somewhere.

I was hooked. There was the general low-budget feel (and look - that was a pretty muddy transfer) of 1970's Italian horror movies. There was the synthesizer music that might or might not fit the scene. There was the over-use of bright-red blood. There was a pretty excruciating eye-impalement (something of a signature for Fulci). There was a zombie fighting a shark. A real shark, mind you. How could I not love it?

The Medium

I've got the Blue Underground Blu-ray release. I almost didn't pick this up, as I wasn't sure *Zombie* was a movie that would benefit from high definition. The poor video quality was part of the charm for me. However there were a bunch of extras on two disks, so I bought it (used).

Man, am I glad I did. The picture quality is improved enough that it almost looks like it's been restored. Colors are bright and the image is sharp and clean (as much as it can be for a low-budget zombie flick, anyway). It was enough to make me revise my opinion of the cinematography, anyway - it's a pretty good looking film now.

The Movie

Zombie has two openings - in the first a shadowy figure points a gun at us (the screen) while drums pound out a tribal beat on the soundtrack. A figure tied into a sheet slowly rises. The gun fires. Blood and brains spurt out of the sheet. The shadowy figure speaks, saying that "the boat can leave now." After the titles we get another opening, wherein an abandoned sailing vessel wanders into New York harbor.

At this point new viewers may be forgiven for thinking there's some depth to the film. We've got a dramatic opening shot - literally - that connects directly to the next sequence and raises all kinds of questions. Is this the same boat? Where did it come from?

What happened to the crew? There's also the chance that maybe the director is deliberately echoing that scene in *Dracula* when the *Demeter* arrives in England with only the captain's corpse aboard.

But no, it's really just an excuse to tie the film to Romero's by shoehorning an opening and a closing sequence in the US. It's effective, though, and the corpulent zombie that attacks New York's Finest is memorable and lets us know we're in for some rough treatment.

We're introduced to two main characters in short order - Peter West, a reporter, and Anne Bowles, the daughter of the owner of the abandoned boat. Ian McCulloch does okay as West - though he's a 70's Hero of the comb-over variety - but Tia Farrow is completely lost as Anne. She spends a good portion of the film staring into the middle distance with a slightly dazed expression. The two are quickly on their way to the Caribbean to try and find Anne's father and hopefully an explanation for what happened on the boat.

Once there they charter a boat, or hijack someone's vacation cruise, I'm not really sure. Anyway, they meet up with another couple and start looking for the island that Anne's father was supposed to be on. The other woman - Susan - goes scuba diving, which leads to that zombie-vs-shark extravaganza I mentioned earlier. Repeated viewing of that scene has dampened some of my amazement, but I remember clearly being bowled over by it the first time. I mean there's a real guy in that zombie makeup under water wrestling with a tiger shark!

Meanwhile, on the island, Dr. Menard is struggling with an outbreak of disease and his wife. She wants to leave, he doesn't - though he's awfully vague about why. He goes to the hospital (after slapping no sense at all into her) where he'll practice medicine via pistol shot (he's the figure in the very first scene). His wife, meanwhile, will take a shower and then get attacked by a zombie. This scene involves an incredibly graphic sequence in which the poor woman's eyeball is pierced by a splinter. It's pretty tough to watch even now.

Our heroes have drive-shaft issues (with the boat, you sicko) and get marooned on the very same island. People run back and forth, there's talk of voodoo and people abandoning villages. Then there are some really gross zombies that may or may not be conquistadors, risen from their graves.

Any real plot has gone out the window long ago, but there's still some really effective shots to be found. A single figure shuffling down the abandoned streets of a village. The red, red blood contrasted with the white, white linens of the hospital. The zombies themselves, all rotting and mud-covered, some with worms dangling out of their eye sockets.

Eventually our heroes are cornered in the hospital and must do battle with ravening hordes of the undead. Things go badly, but not as bad as you might expect, as characters actually survive (though not everyone, of course). The tacked on ending with a horde of zombies making their way across the Brooklyn bridge is surprisingly effective.

The cinematography varies wildly in quality. Much of it is simply workmanlike, with the characters generally in frame and focus. Sometimes, however, Fulci surprises you with shots of almost poetic beauty - the abandoned ship against the old New York skyline (the Trade Center towers looming in the background), dust-blown streets with oddly still figures, zombies shuffling around with their eyes closed like sleepwalkers.

Richard Johnson lends things a bit of gravitas as Dr. Menard, but he's all gravelly voice and darting eyeballs, sweating his way through scenes of vague import. At least his voice fits, unlike some of the other characters, whose dubbing seems half-hearted at best - particularly the second male lead, Brian. Tisa Farrow is so vacant at times that you could almost see one of the characters shooting her as a zombie in the melee - it would be an easy mistake to make.

The Bottom Line

Zombie is an experience. As a horror movie it provides the gore if not the scares - you cringe more than you jump. The barest thread of a plot satisfies only so much as it serves to get the characters to where they can be attacked. But as a Fulci film it satisfies by being a little stylish, a lot gory and a bit crazy.

THE STUFF

"Are you eating it? Or is it eating you?"

Director: Larrry Cohen, Producer: Paul Kurta, Written by: Larry Cohen, Starring: Michael Moriarty, Andrea Marcovicci, Garrett Morris, Paul Sorvino

Larry Cohen, man. *It's Alive*, *Q*, *Maniac Cop*. I even liked *Return to Salem's Lot*. He's a writer with interesting ideas and a director with... well, with tiny budgets. Larry Cohen makes B movies - but they're *interesting* B movies.

The Stuff was one of my favorite horror/comedies in 80's. It was just so ridiculous. Killer yogurt? Kung-fu chocolate chip cookie kings? A racist militia that saves the day? The commercials and the jingle - "Enough is never enough... of The Stuff!"? All solid gold. And there was plenty of gore - though of a particularly bloodless kind.

When Gatorade came out with their "Is it in you?" campaign my brother Jeff and I found this hilarious and he immediately started to refer to it like a The Stuff campaign. This tickles him mightily, even to this day, and I made a quick mockup of an ad for him, with The Stuff logo in place of the Gatorade one.

The Medium

I watched this on Netflix streaming. The quality is okay - and honestly, with a movie like this you're not really paying attention to composition and color quality. I'd still like to see the Arrow Blu-ray release, if only for the commentary.

The Movie

My first reaction upon finding a mysterious white substance

bubbling out of the ground at my mining facility? It would NOT be to taste the damn Stuff. "Say, this stuff tastes real good. Maybe we can sell it to people!" I would have loved to be on the wall of that pitch meeting, "Yeah it comes from the mine tailings, but damn - it's delicious! Just try some... wait, where are you going?"

Somehow this Stuff - which does end up being marketed as The Stuff - passes FDA inspection and becomes a huge commercial success, threatening rival fast-food corporations who hire an industrial saboteur to 'handle' things. This is Mo Rutheford, former FBI agent, played with good-natured dimness by Michael Moriarty. He might not be as dumb as he looks - "Nobody is as dumb as I look" - but he's still not all that bright.

Mo quickly uncovers the truth - that The Stuff is not a low calorie, natural dessert (well, not JUST that). It's actually alive, possibly self-aware, and that it gradually takes over anyone that eats it, devouring them from the inside out. Along the way he manages to convince the ad exec in charge of the The Stuff campaign, Nicole, to help him (mostly by posing as a millionaire oil baron - though she doesn't seem much bothered by his eventual reveal that he's not rich). He also befriends Chocolate Chip Charlie (Garret Morris) who is trying to find out who convinced his relatives to sell his successful cookie business to The Stuff executives.

Meanwhile, a young boy named Jason has seen The Stuff move and is convinced something is wrong. He even destroys a bunch of The Stuff at a local grocery store. His family have succumbed to the evil dessert and try to get him to eat it as well, before Mo shows up and saves the day.

While Charlie heads to Washington DC to warn the FBI, Mo, Nicole and Jason head to the company headquarters to find out what's really going on. This turns out to be nothing less than world domination, as a huge lake of The Stuff is pumped into trucks to be distributed worldwide. Barely escaping with their lives the trio recruits members of a militia to attack the distribution center and spread the word via their radio stations.

In the aftermath, Jason and Mo confront the corporate executives who started the whole thing, delivering a heaping helping of their own product.

Yeah, *The Stuff* is ridiculous, but Cohen embraces the lunacy completely. It doesn't always make sense - in fact it sometimes seems like he was making the movie up as he went along - but it's always fun. The satire is also pretty pointed, even with tongue firmly in cheek. The faux commercials sprinkled throughout the film - featuring some fun cameos - may seem too cheesy and over-the-top now, but they're dead-on perfect parodies of the kind of thing you'd see on TV in 1985.

The dialogue is terrible - when you can hear it - and the cinematography is uninspiring at best, but the effects are often quite good. A scene in which the hotel bed turns out to be full of The Stuff has some great sequences with vast amounts of the liquid spurting around, crawling up walls and catching on fire. Garrett Morris' sequence near the end is crazy gross, both laugh-out-loud funny and gag-inducing.

Morris and Moriarty are great and any scene they're in benefits from their energy and charisma. The child actor is not so good, unfortunately, and Paul Sorvino as the militia captain chews so much scenery you expect there to be bite marks taken out of the walls.

The Bottom Line

There's so much wrong with *The Stuff,* but I love it anyway. It's a movie about a killer dessert. It's got Michael Moriarty. It's got pointed commentary about consumer culture AND Garrett Morris karate chops a guys face off. What's not to love?

BIG ASS SPIDER!

"Let's Do it for the kids!"

Director: Mike Mendez, Producers: Shaked Berenson, Patrick Ewald, Travis Stevens, Klaus von Sayn-Wittgenstein, Written by: Gregory Gieras, Starring: Greg Grunberg, Lombardo Boyar, Ray Wise, Clare Kramer

I remember hearing about *Big Ass Spider!* in 2013 and the title of the film generated a lot of good will on its own - you gotta love when a filmmaker is willing to embrace the cheese in such an up front way. Initial reviews were promising as well, so I've been looking forward to seeing it and was happy to find it on Netflix streaming yesterday.

Maybe I was expecting too much from a film called *Big Ass Spider!*.

The Medium
Netflix streaming, I think I said that already. (The more I do these *31 Days* writeups, the less important the The Medium section seems.) The movie was also released on Blu-ray, which I should probably not be as astonished about as I am. It's got a commentary track, though, with both Grundberg and Boyar, so that might make it worth picking up.

The Movie
Big Ass Spider! starts promisingly with our protagonist Alex (Greg Grunberg) waking up in the middle of a rubble-filled street. He rises and walks forward in slow motion to a Pixies tune, while people run and soldiers fire into the air at something we can't see. Finally the camera tilts to show what he's looking at - it's a big ass spider doing its best King Kong impression on a skyscraper as helicopters buzz around.

Nice! That's an awesome opening and it primes you for what you're expecting will be an epic ride.

The movie then flashes back to the morning of the same day and we're introduced to Alex properly, as a wise-ass but kind-hearted exterminator who's willing to take payment in fruit-cake from an elderly customer. He's bitten by a brown-recluse and ends up at a local hospital where he hits on a nurse (badly) and negotiates to have his bill thrown out if he takes care of a little problem the hospital has. Seems like a large spider is loose in the building...

I'm already concerned at this point. I like Grunberg, but the jokes are pretty flat and the production quality is pretty low.

Alex is teamed up with the security guard, a guy named José (Lombardo Boyar). The jokes get even broader and less funny, though I love José. His half-hearted corrections and asides are the best part of the movie for me. The two actors do work well together, though, and even the crap dialogue can't diminish the obvious fun they're having.

Ray Wise shows up, heading the obligatory military contingent. He's always fun to watch but his character, as with everything in this movie, is overly broad. The military has, in its monster movie way, created the spider and needs to contain it before it reaches the dreaded 'stage 5' (which is reproduction, in case you're wondering). Alex tries his moves on Lieutenant Karly Brant (Clare Kramer), though he's shot down (at first).

Alex and José thrust themselves into the middle of the spider hunt, being as effective (and more so) than the military in tracking and confronting the ever growing spider. There are lots of cameos and gore along the way - including Loyd Kaufman, who gets his face eaten off, and a shot where the spider venom melts a guy. Eventually they find themselves back at the beginning, needing to get into that skyscraper and rescue Karly before the spider's eggs hatch.

The spider effects are inconsistent. Sometimes the armored, alien looking thing is pretty impressive - the skyscraper sequence is particularly well done - and sometimes looks like the worst low-budget CGI effect you can imagine. The jokes are bad, the dialogue is bad, the acting is... also bad, with a few exceptions.

I get the feeling like there's a certain tone the filmmakers are going for and I'm just missing the joke. I know the film is trying to be funny - that it's making fun of a certain kind of film - but it's just too on-the-nose. I'm left feeling like I'm with the guy who keeps elbowing me in the side and going "Isn't that funny? That's funny, right!?" I haven't seen enough SyFy Original Pictures, I guess.

Bottom Line

I would happily watch a show that was just Alex and José running around LA getting into trouble.

It's not that there isn't some fun to be had. I get the feeling like I might enjoy this a lot more with a group of friends. It's just too broad and flat for me. It left me wanting to watch a film with more craft, heart, and subtlety - like *Shaun of the Dead* or *Tucker and Dale vs Evil.*

THE MUMMY (1932)

"Good heavens, what a terrible curse!"

Director: Karl Freund, Producer: Carl Laemmle, Jr., Written by: John L. Balderston, Starring: Boris Karloff, Zita Johann, David Manners, Arthur Byron, Edward van Sloan

It's been a while since I've seen *The Mummy*. It was never one of my favorite Universal monsters, and I think the poor print quality of previous releases has been part of that. My memory of the film is all dark shadows and flickers.

There's also the problem of the Mummy himself - he's only in the movie for maybe five minutes, and most of that time he's motionless in the background. For a kid watching this movie on TV having the title monster not really be part of the festivities was something of a downer. (Yeah, I knew Ardeth Bay was the same guy - and I loved Karloff - but he wasn't the Mummy. He couldn't be - he wasn't wearing bandages!)

I always liked the look of the film, though - especially the Egyptian sequences (in the digs and in flashback). *The Mummy* was created to exploit a huge interest in Egypt and Egyptology that swept the world as a result of the discover and excavation of Tutankhamun's tomb. The world tour of the artifacts from that tomb from 1972-1979 meant another wave of Tut-mania and I was just as caught up in it as anyone else. When I didn't find what I wanted - more of the monster, more Egypt stuff - other Mummy movies supplanted the original in my affections. (Mostly the Hammer pictures.)

The Medium

My wife purchased the *Universal Monsters Essential Blu-ray Collection* for me for my birthday. It's one of my treasures. I've already watched the *Frankenstein* films for previous 31 Days installments - or I'd watch 'em again!

As I mentioned, my memory of earlier *The Mummy* releases were that they were sub-par. I never picked up the Legacy collection, so I don't know if that was a restored version. The Blu-ray is spectacular, however, with an amazing picture quality and great sound as well. Watching the Blu-ray of *The Mummy* is a bit of a revelation, as it's an extremely well-shot film, something I never realized in previous viewings. The extras are okay, with two commentary tracks and a couple of short documentaries as well as a few other things.

The Movie

The Mummy is more melodrama than monster picture, but it's got some horrific moments. The Mummy himself is still sorely lacking, but the moments he's on-screen are great ones. The early scene where he comes to life is still effective and that makeup by Jack Pierce is just incredible. From what I've read it took most of a day to get Karloff into the makeup and another few hours to get him out of it, so perhaps that's why they opted for the Ardeth Bay character instead.

The story is a familiar one now - the resurrected man who finds his ancient love re-incarnated as a modern woman. He then does everything he can to make her remember who she is and return to him. This must have been one of the first times this story was told, though, and it's done very effectively.

The story starts in 1932 in Egypt at an official dig. The mummy of Imhotep, a disgraced priest, is mistakenly brought to life when the Scroll of Thoth is read aloud. Years later he returns posing as a regular Egyptian and points the way to have his beloved Ankh-es-en-amon dug up as well. He intends to use the Scroll to resurrect her in just the same fashion.

Unfortunately for him (and for our heroine) Ankh-es-en-amon has been reincarnated in the person of Helen Grosvenor. He schemes to reawaken her to her past life before killing her and using the Scroll of Thoth to turn her into a deathless mummy like himself.

Karloff is awesome as always, and the repeated closeups of Ardeth Bay and his glowing eyes are pretty creepy. Actually, Bay is creepy *all* the time, standing in weird poses way too close to whoever he is speaking to. Dude has no sense of personal space. This being Karloff the character has more depth than your average monster villain, and you feel for him as he recounts his attempts to resurrect his beloved - only to be tortured and buried alive for his transgression.

Still, his plan calls for killing his beloved and turning her into a monster, so she's pretty distressed. Her rejection of him despite all he's gone through is poignant - but oh so understandable. Zita Johann, the actress who plays Helen/Ankh-es-en-amon is very good for the most part, though she sometimes goes a bit over-the-top. She handles the change in personality between the two characters with skill.

The supporting characters are less memorable, with a modern love interest for Helen and the guy who played Van Helsing in *Dracula* (Edward Van Sloan) as an expert in the occult being the largest roles. There are a few visual effects - a scrying pool being a standout - but it's primarily the makeup and the set design that pop and they're both excellent, especially in this restored version.

The Bottom Line

The Mummy is another reassessed classic for me. It's creepy and melodramatic and fun. The pace is perhaps slower than some of the other Universal Monster pictures - and the paucity of actual Mummy still bothers me a little - but it's a great monster movie anyway.

KILLER CROC DOUBLE FEATURE!

It took a couple of attempts (had to return one copy of *Lake Placid*), but finally got my double bill of crocodilian action going this weekend. There are a ton of horror movies about crocodiles or alligators, but I decided to stick with two I'd seen before and enjoyed. I already watched the awesome *Alligator* last year. Maybe next year we'll try *Black Water* or *Eaten Alive*.

LAKE PLACID
"I'm rooting for the crocodile."

Director: Steve Miner, Producers: David E. Kelley, Michael Pressman, Peter Bogart, Written by: David E. Kelley, Starring: Bill Pullman, Bridget Fonda, Oliver Platt, Brendan Gleeson, Betty White

Movies set in Maine always take a bit more to swallow as a resident. I'm sure this is true of folks who live in other places when they go and see a movie set in their neck of the woods. It's always more remote, more scenic, and more dangerous in the movies. Trying to imagine a lake in Lincoln County that's a mile from the ocean, 25 miles from the nearest town, and that only has one camp on it? That's almost as hard to believe as a 30 foot croc having swum there from Asia. (Also - no brown or grizzly bears in Maine, sorry.) Now if the camp was owned by a rich person from away...

I'm not sure of the exact circumstances that lead to me seeing *Lake Placid* for the first time. I probably decided that the odds on seeing another giant crocodile film in the theater were pretty slim.

I was pleasantly surprised, however, and about the time the deputy has his head chomped off I had completely bought in. Yeah, it was silly - but it was willing to embrace the silliness and toss in a little gore for spice.

I have friends who dislike the movie quite a bit. It was written by David E. Kelly, and I've heard it called "*Ally McBeal* in the Woods." Luckily I've never seen *Ally McBeal*, nor any other David E. Kelly show that I can think of (runs to IMDB). Oh, damn - I did watch *Picket Fences*. But I liked *Picket Fences* too. Ah well, the point is none of the stuff that seems to bother them - the woman angry about a relationship breakup (that sounds like a bad relationship anyway), the wacky characters defined mostly by quirks and bon mots - none of that stuff bothers me. I dunno, maybe I was distracted by the giant crocodile.

The Medium

I ended up watching this via Amazon streaming. The only copies the local Bull Moose had were either Full Screen or the new Blu-ray. I like the movie, but not enough to fork out Blu-ray money for it. I'd purchased a Full Screen copy without realizing it and decided to return it, rather than deal with pan-and-scan. (I used the money from the return to pick up *Cloverfield* and *[REC]*, so it wasn't a complete waste of time.)

The picture quality was good - it's been consistently better on Amazon than on Netflix lately. There are some decent shots, particularly of the lake, so it was nice to have a good quality stream.

The Movie

A biologist studying beavers (shut up) in a remote Maine lake is savagely attacked and bitten in half (he's pretty lively for all that - at least for a few moments). The local authorities ask for an expert from New York to examine a tooth that's been recovered from the body and the museum sends Kelly Scott (Bridget Fonda). Kelly isn't exactly a fan of fieldwork, but she's willing to go to get away from a co-worker with whom she's had a bad breakup. She gets to Maine and examines the tooth where she quickly identifies it.

Guess what it is. Go on, guess.

Sheriff Keogh (Brendan Gleeson) and Game Warden Jack Wells (Bill Pullman) aren't sure the snarky (and somewhat flaky) paleontologist is correct, but they head to the lake to investigate. They're quickly joined by Hector Cyr (Oliver Platt), an eccentric mythology expert who thinks that crocodiles are godly.

God, this really does sound stupid, doesn't it?

It all somehow works, though. The comedic bits and character interactions are all balanced by crocodile attacks and some pretty salty language from Betty White. She plays Mrs. Bickerman, the only resident of the lake and someone who readily admits to killing her husband while hiding the fact that she also knows about the monstrous crocodile. She's awesome. And really foul-mouthed. In 1999 I was not expecting that from the Golden Girl, so it made me giggle each time she muttered "cocksuckers."

The crocodile attacks are all well done and are generally suspenseful. The bit where the poor deputy is decapitated in a swim-by attack got a loud laugh from me in the theater, earning me several dismayed looks from my fellow audience members.

Pullman and Fonda are honestly a bit vanilla in their roles. Pullman in particular sometimes looks like he's only there for the paycheck. Gleeson and Platt are pretty good, though, and their dynamic provides most of the fun as far as human characters go.

In typical giant "nature attacks" fashion an overly complicated plan to take the croc alive is hatched, leading to some fun with helicopters and cows in slings ("She looks like an enormous teabag.") Surprisingly, the monster survives the final encounter and is last seen headed down-state on a flatbed. (I haven't seen the sequels to this movie - of which there are two - but I would hope the next one starts off with the croc breaking free from the flatbed on Interstate 95 around, say, Worcester.)

The Bottom Line

It's not going to be for everyone, but there's plenty of fun to be had in *Lake Placid*. There are quirky characters, action-packed set pieces and the occasional decapitation. I didn't expect much when I first saw it and was pleasantly surprised. Go in with low expectations and you might be surprised as well.

ROGUE
"What did you think of the tour?"

Director: Greg McLean, Producers: Matt Hearn, David Lightfoot, Greg McLean, Written by: Greg McLean, Starring: Michael Vartan, Radha Mitchell, Sam Worthington

This is an altogether different film, though the basics are the same: disparate group of characters is menaced by enormous crocodile. There is some humor, but it is primarily a serious monster movie. It's one of the better "nature attacks" films I've seen, and I'd put it up there with *Alligator* as one of my top two crocodilian films.

Holy crap. I have a top ten list of crocodilian films.

I first saw *Rogue* on a whim. It was on Netflix streaming and I'd heard nothing but good things about the director's previous film, *Wolf Creek*. I enjoyed it immensely and was surprised at the overall level of quality.

The Medium

I bought the 'Unrated' DVD release of *Rogue* specifically for *31 Days*. It looks pretty sharp, even on the big TV. I have no idea what was added to make this 'Unrated' - it seems substantially the same as the version I saw on streaming. (It's possible it *was* this version, come to think of it.) There are a handful of extras, including a making-of documentary and a commentary track. There is a Blu-ray release, but there are no extras on the US version.

The Movie

A travel writer, Pete (Michael Vartan) joins a group of tourists on a crocodile viewing river cruise. Although there's a short encounter with some locals, the trip is mostly a pleasant diversion. When they are about to turn around and head back one of the tourists sees a distant distress flare. The boat operator and guide, Kate (Radha Mitchell) informs them that they'll have to check it out - despite the fact that she can't raise her base on the radio.

The characters are all quickly and economically presented - Pete is a world weary snob, Kate is the pretty-but-tough local who loves the land, there's the camera-nerd/jackass, the family with an ill member, the pushy housewife and others. It's all done fairly well and there are even moments that have a certain depth to them. One character quietly releases ashes into the river, observed only by the girl whose mother is sick. She turns and hugs her mother tightly. It sounds maudlin, but it was a lovely bit.

The movie is packed with recognizable actors. Michael Vartan was in *Alias* (and, in a bit of synchronicity, in a couple of episodes of *Ally McBeal* as well). Radha Mitchell was in *Pitch Black* and *Silent Hill* amongst other things. Sam Worthington plays one of the local toughs. There was a male actor who I knew I should recognize but just couldn't place until he'd been eaten - turns out he's Robert Taylor who starred in the Netflix series *Longmire* (as well has having played Agent Jones in *The Matrix*). And of course there's John Jarratt, who played Mick Tayler in *Wolf Creek*.

Eventually the boat finds a secluded area of the river and is immediately attacked by a huge crocodile. They wreck the boat on a small island, which wouldn't be so bad if it wasn't in a tidal river. Eventually the tide is going to come in and they'll all be at the mercy of the croc.

It's a standard 'nature attacks' story, isolating a group of strangers and watching them struggle with the monster and each other. It's done extremely well here, though. There's real tension and scares to be had and the director, Greg McLean, does the smart thing by keeping the croc hidden or revealed only in pieces for much of the movie. There's a scene where the survivors are arguing about something and there's a splash. They all turn to find one of their number (who was standing too close to the river edge) is gone - you only see the barest glimpse of a huge tail disappearing beneath the water. The guy didn't even get a chance to scream. Where that sort of scene would have been played for laughs in *Lake Placid* it's all serious business here.

I appreciated the fact that no one is a complete asshole. People do stupid, selfish things as the tension mounts, but they're understandable in context. Even the 'hero' is only put in the position to save someone by accident - he slips and falls into the croc's lair. All the actors do a good job, with no one standing out as a weak link.

The monster effects are top-notch when finally shown and the croc is scary as hell. The cinematography is also to be commended, with some of the most spectacular footage of the Australian countryside that I've ever seen. It might be full of killer crocs, but it sure made me want to go visit anyway.

The Bottom Line

Rogue is a top notch monster movie of the 'oversized predator attacks' variety. It's above average in pacing, writing, acting, effects, and cinematography. If you see only one giant crocodilian movie, this is the one to see.

THIRTEEN GHOSTS
(2001)

"Of course this basement! What is it with you people? If it was the basement next door I wouldn't give a shit, would I?"

Director: Steve Beck, Producers: Robert Zemeckis, Joel Silver, Gilbert Adler, Written by: Neal Marshall Stevens, Richard D'Ovidio, Starring: Tony Shalhoub, Embeth Davidtz, Matthew Lillard, Shannon Elizabeth, F. Murray Abraham

I'm starting to feel like all my choices this October are guilty pleasures rather than good films. Certainly *Thirteen Ghosts* falls into the category. It's not a good film, per-se, but it's fun and has some awesome monsters.

Dark Castle made a handful of remakes of classic horror films in the late 90's/early 2000's. We got *The House on Haunted Hill, Thirteen Ghosts* and *House of Wax*. I'd never seen the original *13 Ghosts*, so I was able to go in without any expectations and enjoy it. (*House of Wax*, on the other hand... gah.)

The Medium
I have the DVD release, which is, like the film itself, serviceable. It's got a commentary track, which I actually didn't expect. There's a documentary and some 'Ghost Profiles.' It also comes from that time when "Interactive Menus" were something that got listed in the Special Features on the back of the DVD case.

The Movie
I still haven't seen the William Castle movie, so I'm not sure how

closely the film hews to the original. If it's anything like *The House on Haunted Hill* it'll only be in the general outlines. A strange man (F. Murray Abraham) who collects ghosts dies and leaves his house to his nephew, Arthur (Tony Shaloub). The nephew and his family go to inspect the house, which is an insane thing made mostly of glass. Oh, and the basement is full of ghosts in cages. Really creepy, scary ghosts.

One thing you have to give this movie is the production quality, which is top notch. The ghosts are fantastic - gory and frightening - and the house itself is a masterpiece of crazy, with sliding glass walls, clockwork machines and weird knickknacks in every corner. Even as the threadbare plot unfolds - something to do with opening a portal to hell I think - the ghosts and the house provide plenty of visual and visceral entertainment.

Soon after the family arrives a machine in the basement is triggered which both seals the house and starts releasing the ghosts. These aren't your regular, harmless apparitions either - they're all murderous spirits whose body count has only increased in the afterlife. Trapped in the house with the family is the man that helped capture all those ghosts, Dennis (Matthew Lillard), and while the family may not have a clue he knows exactly what kind of danger they're in.

One of the gimmicks of *Thirteen Ghosts* is that the only way to see the ghosts is through special glasses. This is a neat little touch that provides some of the (many) jump scares in the film. It's also how Dennis convinces the others that there's a danger.

The film after that point is basically a series of chase sequences/ghost attacks as the family searches for the youngest boy and a way out. There's a plot about the house being a machine that's powered by ghosts in order to open a path to hell, or a portal to immortality or something - I'm pretty vague on the details, even after having seen it a couple of times. The bottom line is that there are twelve ghosts and a thirteenth ghost might have the ability to stop the machine - meaning someone in the party has to die.

Another thing that surprises me each time is the level of gore in this film. The production quality is uniformly high and they were able to afford decent actors, so you expect the producers to be pushing for a PG-13 rating to get more teenagers into the theater. Not in *Thirteen Ghosts*. There's a scene involving a lawyer who is literally cut in half - the long way - and they keep the camera focused on him as the two halves slowly separate. There's also a ghost who is a woman that committed suicide (after botching her own plastic surgery) - she's terrifying. There's a scene in which the daughter (Shannon Elizabeth) gleefully uses the bathroom while that ghost also uses the mirror and sits in a tub full of blood - of course without the glasses the daughter sees none of this, but we're able to see it in awful detail.

All the ghosts have a designation. There's The Torso, The Juggernaut, The Torn Prince, and The Jackal amongst others. Really, they're the reason to see the film, as the makeup effects are just great.

The cinematography is pretty good, especially given how much of a nightmare it must have been for the lighting and camera folks to try and get decent angles in a house made of glass. The acting is serviceable and this is one of the first films where I can actually tolerate Matthew Lillard. Tony Shalhoub is also good, if a little understated, and F. Murray Abraham is always good value. The others aren't standouts, but they aren't bad.

The Bottom Line

Along with *The House on Haunted Hill*, *Thirteen Ghosts* is one of the few recent remakes of classic horror films that isn't actively terrible (I'm looking at you *House of Wax* and *The Fog*). It's not great - it might even be a stretch to call it good - but it's fun and has some great production values.

C.H.U.D.

"I saw it on TV."

Director: Douglas Cheek, Producer: Andrew Bonime, Written by: Parnell Hall, Starring: John Heard, Daniel Stern, Christopher Curry, Kim Greist

C.H.U.D. was a staple of my horror viewing in the 80's. I must have seen it fifteen or twenty times. Even now I'm not sure exactly what it is about the film that was so entertaining. Don't get me wrong - it's full of low-budget monster-movie fun - but there were plenty of other horror films in the 80's that could have made it into heavy rotation on the VCR but didn't.

Having seen it so often, *C.H.U.D.* became like a shorthand for discussing horror movies. "Better than *C.H.U.D.*" could mean that it was actually a good movie or it could mean it was so bad it became fun. "Worse than *C.H.U.D.*" was something you really did not want to be watching.

I used to have a VHS copy of the movie, but that's disappeared. I gave a bunch of my horror movie tapes to my brother Scott when I switched to DVD, so it's possible he still has them. One of these days I'll have to pick up a copy again. (Criterion once posted that they would be releasing a special edition on Blu-ray with a ton of extras but, alas, this turned out to be an April Fools' Day prank.)

C.H.U.D. is also the archetypal "good actor in a bad film" movie - with John Heard the nominal star. I think this was also the first movie I ever saw John Goodman in. Daniel Stern was probably the bigger name at the time the movie was made, though, having done *Breaking Away* and *Diner.* I was just looking at the IMDB entry for the movie and was surprised to see Christopher Curry - Captain

Bosch - is in one of my wife's favorite shows, *Hart of Dixie*. (I've never been able to watch it, myself.)

The Medium

In the absence of a DVD, I watched *C.H.U.D.* on Netflix streaming. Arrow video released an 'extensively restored' Blu-ray with a bunch of extras, including both the theatrical and 'integral' cuts of the film. As much as it seems weird to own a high definition version of such a classically gritty film, I'll probably have to track this down.

The Movie

C.H.U.D. opens with a creature attacking a woman out walking her dog. It's late at night, the street is filthy and litter-strewn and slightly damp. As she passes by a manhole a leathery, taloned hand reaches out and grabs her. Then we're treated to the longest sequence involving a street sweeper in modern cinema. I mean it seems to last at least as long as that fight scene in *They Live*. The vehicle passes by several homeless people before finally sweeping over the manhole and the woman's shoe - the only thing that remains.

There are two storylines in *C.H.U.D.* - one follows a photographer, Cooper(Heard), who has foregone a fashion industry career to document a segment of the homeless population who live underground. He even helps bail out one of them, a woman named Mrs. Munroe who tried to steal a cops pistol. He follows her underground to talk to her brother - who rants about being attacked by creatures before showing Cooper his leg, which has been severely bitten.

The other storyline involves a Police Captain named Bosch (first name Heironymous?) who has been ordered to ignore the increase in disappearances in his precinct. Once his wife becomes one of the missing, however, Bosch hooks up with "The Reverend" Shepherd (Stern), a man who runs a soup kitchen and has been reporting a large number of them as missing, particularly those who live underground. Together they confront authorities - including a member of the Nuclear Regulatory Commision - with evidence pointing to... *something* happening underground. They're laughed out of the room of course, but it turns out there IS something down there that's snacking on the homeless. It's a Cannibalistic Humanoid Underground Dweller - a C.H.U.D.!

Man, I forgot how grimy this movie is. It's very much an 80's horror film, but it sometimes feels like a throwback to the 70's. Everything looks like it's decaying and falling apart. The streets are always damp and there's trash and graffiti everywhere. I almost expect to see The Warriors walking through on their way back to Coney Island. Even the social commentary - the real bad guys are, of course, the government - feels like it's from an earlier time.

The monsters, when we finally see them (which takes way too long), are fairly decent, especially for such a small budget film. The glowing eyes are a nice touch and I wish they'd made more use of them, with lots of glowing eyes appearing in darkness or showing in the background of a dim scene.

There's a lot of crazy in this movie. The NRC guy puts a tail on Shepherd and, to intimidate him, the guy swallows a quarter. That's it. He swallows a quarter. Later on this guy - in Izod shirt and Aviator sunglasses - locks Shepherd underground and I thought, "what, was he carrying a shiny new padlock with him the whole time?" There's the C.H.U.D. that attacks Cooper's wife Lauren (Kim Greist), ignoring everyone else in the building and then growing a super-long neck for no reason I can tell. It does make it easier for her to chop its head off with the sword that is conveniently hung on the wall.

That's part of the fun, though. It doesn't have to make sense. Would the NYPD used flamethrowers underground, where pockets of methane sometimes accumulate? Probably not, but who cares? There are monsters to be had, there's toxic waste and gunfights and chase scenes in the sewer. C.H.U.D.s even attack a diner (bringing the problem to the attention of the rest of the city) - though unfortunately we don't get to see that attack. I really wanted to see John Goodman and Jay Thomas struggling with the rubber monsters.

By the time we get to the finale, with gas flooding the sewers and Cooper and Shepherd trapped underground with a horde of C.H.U.D.s, you've either full committed to the insanity or you've moved on to another movie with higher production values, like *Street Trash*, maybe. The ending does disappoint a bit - I really wanted to see manhole covers exploding into the air like in *Alligator* - but the whole movie is a bit of an up-and-down experience. There are moments of low-budget joy, like when the C.H.U.D.s all line up outside the diner, window shopping for their next meal. But these are often followed by moments of disappointment, like the attack on the cops and the NRC guys in the sewer - screams and a screen going to static? Way to cheap out, guys - give us some gore!

The Bottom Line

I don't know if I can recommend *C.H.U.D.*, but I love it anyway. It's grimy and falling apart and barely makes sense (not unlike some of the actors), but it's still a B-movie gem. It's gory and funny and weirdly earnest. I can't tell you *why* I like it, just that I do.

THE UNINVITED (1944)

"They call them the haunted shores…"

Director: Lewis Allen, Producer: Charles Brackett, Written by: Frank Partos, Dodie Smith, Starring: Ray Milland, Ruth Hussey, Donald Crisp, Cornelia Otis Skinner, Gail Russell

I rented *The Uninvited* from Netflix assuming that I'd never seen it before - I'd been eyeing the Criterion Collection DVD for a while, but it was completely based on the film's reputation as one of the first to treat ghosts in a straightforward fashion. (Up until *The Uninvited* the ghost was primarily used in comedies and was most often a gag or hoax.) I couldn't quite bring myself to buy a film sight unseen, however, especially at Criterion prices. When we re-upped our DVD subscription this was one of the first movies on the list - I could finally see this classic!

Unfortunately, as the movie started with the brother and sister (Ray Milland and Ruth Hussey) approaching a huge house on a cliff top, I realized that I HAD seen the movie before. Seen it, and been unimpressed. It was long enough ego that I couldn't actually remember when I'd seen it, though. Perhaps on one of those Saturday afternoons at Gram's that I've mentioned a few times.

I turned the DVD off and paced the basement for a few minutes. This was actually the second movie I'd received from Netflix erroneously thinking I hadn't seen it (the other was Argento's *The Bird With The Crystal Plumage*) and I was annoyed with myself. I thought about just looking for something else, either in the collection or on Netflix, but I'd had a long day and wasn't much in the mood to go trawling. I'd been looking forward to a good old-fashioned ghost story as well.

Time ticked by. Finally, disgusted with my own indecision, I turned the machine back and sat down to watch. I wasn't looking forward to it anymore, but it was better than dithering.

The Medium

The Criterion DVD is good, looking sharp on my screen even though it's not HD quality. Unlike some recent DVDs I've gotten from Netflix this one had a few extras on it - including a 'pictorial essay' which is as boring as it sounds.

The Movie

The Uninvited follows a pair of siblings, Rick and Pamela Fitzgerald. On a vacation together in Cornwall they stumble across an abandoned cliffside house. Taken with the resemblance to their own childhood residence they inquire about it with the owner, Commander Beech. In short order they purchase it for an extremely low price.

During the transaction they meet the Commander's granddaughter Stella (Gail Russell) who is very upset at the sale. The house (called Windward House) was once her mother's and she feels it is the last connection she has with her, it being the place where her mother died. Stella's grandfather has forbidden her to visit the place, but she's invited to do so by Rick, who is attracted to her. He also tries to get her to shake off her conformity by going sailing with him.

At this point I was still pretty unhappy with things and the general tone - more romantic comedy than spookfest - wasn't making me feel much better. I think my mood allowed me to disregard things that were already slightly off in the film - the locked door at the top of the stairs, the weird insistence by the Commander about Stella staying away from Windward. Still, I soldiered on.

Things do get more spooky after the Fitzgerald's purchase the house. While most of the house is fine the locked room turns out to be a study with a distinctly chilly air. (Aesthetically, it's one of the most beautiful sets, so it was difficult to buy it as being an awful room.) In fact, the room seems to suck all the joy and energy out of anyone who enters it - both Rick and Pamela are almost overcome with ennui. So of course Rick chooses it as his study, where he'll write music!

The night Rick returns from London (where he goes almost immediately after the purchase of the house - leaving Pamela to start renovating) he awakens to the sound of a woman sobbing and moaning. Assuming it's his sister or the housekeeper he creeps out into the hall. When his sister also comes into the hall she informs him that there's a ghost in the house. Rick, trying to be sensible, insists there has to be a rational explanation. Sure buddy. Sure there is.

Stella comes to visit for dinner at Rick's express invitation and she senses a spirit, which she assumes is her mother due to the strong accompanying scent of mimosa, her mother's favorite perfume. Overcome by some force she dashes for the cliff before Rick saves her at the last second. She has no memory of the event.

Okay, things are starting to pick up here. The ghost moaning is pretty creepy and it's fun to watch Rick's face as he tries to convince himself that there's nothing supernatural going on. The sudden flight by Stella towards the cliff is startling as well. Things get more interesting as the town doctor, Dr. Scott (Alan Napier) gets involved. First he helps with Stella and then gives the Fitzgeralds some more background info on how her mother died.

Seems Stella's father, a painter, had an affair with a gypsy woman named Carmel. Stella's mother, Mary Meredith, took Carmel to Paris and left her there. At some point Carmel returned and, during a struggle, flung Mary Meredith from the cliff. She died herself not long after.

Now we're entering gothic romance territory! This movie is getting better all the time. Soon they're throwing a fake séance to try and break Stella's unnatural attraction to the place, but it all goes awry of course, with the glass moving by itself and Stella being possessed by a spirit and talking in Spanish.

The Commander gets wind of all this and responds by sending Stella to a sanitarium run by a woman named Miss Holloway - who turns out to have once been a friend of Mary Meredith. The Fitzgeralds and Dr. Scott continue their investigations, even interviewing Miss Hollaway while unaware that Stella has been imprisoned on the premises.

Things build from there with conspiracies, TWO ghosts, and a frightening climactic confrontation at Windward. I don't want to give too much away, even though it's been 60 years since the film came out. I saw the twists coming, but they're fun and I don't want to spoil anything for folks who haven't seen it.

The cinematography is excellent and on the whole the film is really well made, with good pacing, sets and acting. The special effects are few, but they're effective when used. I usually like Ray Milland a lot - even in low-budget films like *Frogs* - but he's a little stiff here. I would have loved to see Jimmy Stewart in the same role, as I think he would have had more energy and range. Still, Rick is likeable and his expressions really are priceless sometimes. Ruth Hussey is great and Gail Russell is just stunning.

The Bottom Line

I must have been in a mood the first time I saw *The Uninvited*, because it's very good. Yes, it's a melodrama and there's plenty of romantic shenanigans, but there's also some atmospheric spookiness and good, old-fashioned ghost action as well. I ended up liking it quite a bit.

SCANNERS

"We're gonna do this the scanner way."

Director: David Cronenberg, Producer: Claude Héroux, Written by: David Cronenberg, Starring: Jennifer O'Neill, Stephen Lack, Patrick McGoohan, Michael Ironside

Scanners, man. **Scanners**.

Scanners is the only movie that gave me nightmares from just the TV spot. It's not even that scary of a commercial, but somehow it got to me. I remember the nightmare in detail even now, probably because bad dreams don't usually fill me with the horrible sense of dread I got during that particular one.

It'll sound stupid, but here's the dream: I'm sitting in a chair in an all white room. In front of me is a front-loading dryer, which is also white. Behind and to the left of the machine is a doorway to a white hall that I can only make out because the light in the hall is slightly dimmer than the light in the room. In the dryer, slowly tumbling and making sounds like a steak sizzling on a pan, is a piece of meat. Not like a steak or something innocuous like that - it's obviously an organ of some kind, like a liver or a pancreas - something I can't immediately recognize, but just know came from inside a person. And for no reason at all I'm absolutely terrified by this piece of tumbling meat. Suddenly I see someone walk by outside the doorway - it's the guy from the commercial, the guy who looks kinda like Frank Oz (the guy whose head explodes, actually, but I didn't know that when I had the nightmare). I try and call out to him, but I can't speak. The door to the dryer is going to open soon. The organ - whatever it is, all red and leathery - will stop tumbling.

I don't know what's going to happen then, but whatever it is will be awful.

And then I woke up. See? Dumb dream. Still gives me a minor sense of dread just thinking about it, though.

If you really want to see it, this is the TV spot on YouTube: http://tinyurl.com/y2cp5dg8 (as of 2019).

When I finally did see the movie it was nowhere near as scary as my dream. It was, however, the coolest psychic powers movie I had ever seen. Watching it now you'll find that it's very slow and talky and most of the psychic stuff involves closeups of people who look like they're having a gas attack, but at the time it was frackin' amazing. That scene where Vale is basically hacking a computer with his mind and the bad guys shut the link off? In my head that shit was up there with *Star Wars* in awesomeness.

I spent a good part of the eighties obsessed with psychic powers in movies and fiction. The first comic book character I created was a telekinetic. The second or third short story I ever wrote was about a guy who developed psychic powers and used them to kill the kids that were bullying him at school. (I would probably get suspended or expelled for writing something like that in school nowadays.) I can lay that fascination directly at *Scanners'* door - and it's a movie I re-watched a lot back then.

One last tangent (yeah, right) about my experience with the movie. The first time I watched it I loved it, but I was initially very confused. For some reason I had gotten it into my head that the movie was an adaptation of "Scanners Live in Vain" by Cordwainer Smith (which I still think would make a great movie). Took several minutes to adjust my expectations.

The Medium
I picked up the Criterion Collection Blu-ray release of *Scanners*, and it's fantastic. The transfer itself is top notch - the best the movie has ever looked by far. It's not going to be as clean or detailed looking as a more modern movie - there's a significant amount of grain in certain scenes, for instance - but it looks very sharp. I've read reviews by some folks who have a problem with the color tone, which has a distinctly greenish cast, but it doesn't bother me.

There are quite a few extras, including trailers, interviews and Cronenberg's first feature-length film, *Stereo* (which I'm looking forward to watching at some point). No commentary track, which is a little disappointing.

The packaging is nice, with an illustration theme that runs throughout the set. I personally like the art style (by Connor Willumsen) a lot, but it's an individual taste thing. The slipcase also includes a pamphlet with an essay by Kim Newman.

The Movie

Scanners is a movie about people with a special ability called 'scanning.' It's a little like telepathy, but as described in the movie it's "the ability to connect two nervous systems separated by space." A scanner with enough power can read thoughts, speed up a heartbeat, control someone's actions, and even kill. There's also a telekinetic element and even some pyrokinesis - this stuff seems to fall out of the given definition of scanning, but it's all psychic powers, right? Right.

The movie follows a character named Cameron Vale (Stephen Lack) as he goes from homeless person to psychic spy. He's hauled out of being a transient after mentally assaulting an older lady in a shopping mall. He explains his attack by saying something like "she made me do it by thinking about me." There's all kinds of space in that statement to follow up - is it the abuser's "she made me do it" cry? Is there something about being an untrained scanner that means your mind is easily sucked in by those around you? Does an intense 'thought' provoke an intense response in a scanner? The attack looks deliberate to me, so that "she made me" defense reveals a certain flaw in Vale's character if you look at it that way. None of those things are followed up on - it's just a throwaway line - but it's interesting to think about.

Cameron finds himself tied to a bed, dressed in white clothes, while a distinguished looking man in glasses (and black clothes) proceeds to psychically torture him with a crowd of people. Eventually the man, Dr. Paul Ruth (Patrick McGoohan) gives Cameron a drug called Ephemerol that dampens his abilities, allowing him to hear himself think for the first time. I'm not sure what the torture session was supposed to accomplish. It goes on way too long for it to be simply a way to show how effective the drug is (this is one of the scenes that slows the pace down a significant amount). It really does feel like Dr. Ruth (yeah, I know) is purposefully torturing Cameron, breaking him down to the point that the relief the drug offers engenders a sense of gratitude to his torturer.

Meanwhile, a company called ConSec is giving a demonstration - revealing to a select group of people that scanners exist and what they can do. The demonstration goes horribly awry however when the volunteer in the audience turns out to be a scanner himself, Darryl Revok (Michael Ironside). This leads up to that infamous head-explosion scene.

As a horror movie fan and a gore fan (though more in my teens and twenties than now), that head explosion was always the one against which any other gore effect was measured. It's just truly startling in its realism and graphic nature. It also occurs early enough in the movie to be a calling card - letting the audience know what they're in for. One of the extras reveals that this scene was originally intended to lead off the film, but that test audiences simply could not get past that moment to engage with the rest of the movie. Though nothing else in the film aspires to the same level of visceral (and viscera) disgust, the original placement colored the entire experience.

The movie goes on to pit Revok and Vale against each other. Cameron tries to infiltrate a group of scanners in order to get access to Revok and stop him from killing or subsuming all other known scanners. Along the way he finds a group of unaffiliated scanners, including Kim Obrist (Jennifer O'Neill), but Revok seems to always be just one step behind, attacking and killing everyone Cameron comes into contact with.

With Kim's help Cameron finally infiltrates Revok's company, only to find that things are a lot more complicated than they at first appeared - Revok may be working for ConSec - or perhaps it's ConSec that's working for him. Either way, Revok's plan, a program called Ripe, is a massive conspiracy to create more scanners - and Dr. Ruth may be involved.

On the run from both Revok and ConSec, Vale attempts to download the information about Ripe by scanning the ConSec computer remotely. Security attempts to wipe the computer drive - and Vale - with explosive results.

This is still an awesome sequence, 80's phone connection and tape drives and all. As things go bad and stuff starts to explode on both sides of the connection I'm always filled with a level of uncomfortable glee - "that's what you get for messing with a scanner, asshole!" Small details like melted plastic running out of the phone mouthpiece as just fantastic. And if an exploding telephone booth is a bit goofy? Ah well - psychic powers, right? Whattaya gonna do?

Armed with the computer info, Vale and Kim uncover the truth about Ripe and Revok's plan, leading to a final confrontation from which neither Vale nor Revok will emerge unscathed.

The veins! The flames! It's a fantastic set piece. I hadn't known that Dick Smith had worked on this film - he's the guy who did makeup for *The Exorcist* and *The Godfather*, amongst others (his last film was apparently the remake of *The House on Haunted Hill*). There was a team of effects guys on this film, but a lot of this final confrontation was created by him.

Watching the film this time around, the creepiest part of the movie to me is the long-range plans of Revok. This is a man who is planning generations down the line. He's seeding the population with scanners and planning on culling and harvesting them into an army. He's got lists that include doctors and patient names and addresses and is willing to put time and effort and inhuman patience into his plan.

I also still really like the way the powers are portrayed. Scanning is not some easy, twitch-reaction thing. It takes time to make the connection, effort and concentration to accomplish any effect. It looks painful and difficult. Yeah, there are a few too many shots of shaking jowls and rolling eyeballs, but it's still effective stuff. Before that guy's head explodes you can feel the pressure building in his skull.

The movie is let down in a couple of spots. The pacing is off, with some parts being glacially slow and others being over before they have a real chance to get good. Vale's 'indoctrination' via crowd torture goes on way too long and his 'Rocky Training' moment with a yoga master is over almost before it begins. I think some of this can be attributed to the on-the-fly nature of the screenwriting process - Cronenberg was literally writing the movie as he went, sometimes even changing things on-set.

The biggest issue with the movie, though, is the lead. Stephen Lack's surname seems appropriate, as there is definitely something lacking in his performance. I actually think this absence of affect is intentional - Cameron is someone who has literally never had a moment in which to develop his own personality, so of course he's a bit of a cipher, a bit flat. It's not always enjoyable to watch, however, no matter how much I identified with him as a teen.

The other performances are much more enjoyable, with Michael Ironside always worth the price of admission and Patrick McGoohan providing much needed gravitas to all his scenes. Jennifer O'Neill often looks a bit lost, but she balances that out with some very effective 'Blue Steel' looks as she 'scans' people.

The soundtrack by Howard Shore is great, with a lot of dissonant electronic chords and isolated piano keys. The theme music is appropriately bombastic and distinctive and adds a certain gothic atmosphere to the scenes in which it plays.

The Bottom Line

Scanners is an old favorite that, for me, holds up even now. It's got its rough spots - uneven pacing, a lackluster star - but it's still a classic. Every time I watch it I find new things to enjoy and think about.

EVIL DEAD (2013)

"You're all going to die tonight."

Director: Fede Álvarez, Producers: Robert Tapert, Sam Raimi, Bruce Campbell, Written by: Fede Álvarez, Rodo Sayagues, Starring: Jane Levy, Shiloh Fernandez, Lou Taylor Pucci, Jessica Lucas, Elizabeth Blackmore

As a huge fan of the original movie I was looking forward to this with both anticipation and trepidation. How do you remake such an iconic film? Having Sam Raimi, Rob Tapert, and Bruce Campbell on board as producers help alleviate my concerns somewhat, but I still worried - what if it was awful? Or even worse, what if it was just mediocre? What if it bombed at the box office, killing any chance of future *Evil Dead/Army of Darkness* movies?

Man, I put a lot of baggage on this movie.

Regardless, I planned on seeing it in the theater, preferably on opening night, hopefully with a bunch of *Evil Dead* fans. And then I suddenly didn't care about horror movies any more. I just hit a burnout point. For the first time in my life I didn't have any interest in horror. None. For me this was akin to suddenly getting bored with breathing. It was traumatic and disconcerting to have such an integral part of my self-identity just be GONE. This went on for months and months - most of 2013, actually. So the release date for *Evil Dead* came and went and I stayed home.

The burnout passed, thank goodness, and I got back into the swing of things in time for October 2013, but I'd missed *Evil Dead*. And I kept missing it. There always seemed to be something else to watch, some other movie I'd missed or wanted to see. It started to become a thing - when was I going to watch the remake of *The Evil Dead*?

I mean, the reviews were mixed, but not bad. And it sounded really gory, all done with practical effects - I mean, I love that stuff.

Well, finally this September I found a cheap copy of the DVD and decided I had see it, HAD to see it, at least for *31 Days*. Good, bad or indifferent, pull the bandage off and get it over with.

The Medium

I picked up the DVD. Somehow couldn't bring myself to buy the Blu-ray, which was dumb. The cinematography is so good I think the Blu-ray would be worth it. Maybe eventually. The picture was fairly decent, although quick moving scenes had some substantial blur - not sure if that's source material, the DVD or my television. There are a handful of extras, which I still appreciate on a DVD that's not a special edition or anything. No commentary, though - that's a Blu-ray exclusive.

The Movie

Right off the bat I'm torn. The opening sequence, in which a girl is chased through the woods, captured and taken to a horrific basement, is pretty riveting. It's atmospheric, tense and really well shot. The confrontation between her and her father, the appearance of the Naturon Demonto, the deformed people - it's all good horror stuff. It's also a gut puncher, with fire and shotgun breaking familial bonds.

And yet... it's exposition. It's explanation. It shows how the Book gets in the basement (as well as all those dead cats). It's well done - but I was a little annoyed. Yeah, there is an explanation in the earlier films, but I think the film might have been better without it. How much creepier would all that stuff be without explanation - burnt pillar, dead cats, book in plastic and barbed wire? Knowing something horrible happened, but not exactly what? Just letting us infer what happened from Eric's reading of the book?

I got the feeling sometimes like the director was uncertain of his audience's ability to pay attention. There's a moment when Eric (Lou Taylor Pucci) and David (Shiloh Fernandez) are exploring the basement and we first see the charred pillar and there's a sudden flashback to the burning girl from the opening and I was immediately annoyed again. WE KNOW what happened, you don't have to remind us, it's been like fifteen minutes. I got that same feeling several times, like the director was concerned that we'd forgotten things or gotten bored.

You know, I'm starting off with negative things, and I don't want to give the impression that I didn't like the film. I did, actually, I liked it a lot. For most of the movie I was enjoying things and impressed with the quality of the production and especially the effects - some of those gore set pieces are amazing. I still have no idea how they did that bit with the girl's face.

In fact, for most of the initial setup I was pretty happy. There are nods to the original without them being annoying. The 'Classic' is a wreck under a pile of leaves in the yard, for instance. There's a sequence as the car arrives that includes a quick shot of the bench swing and I expected the sound of it banging against the wall - and I was pleased when it didn't come. I liked that the setup was different - it's a bunch of kids coming to the cabin to help their friend (and sister) go cold turkey from heroin. What a great way to ignore that character when she starts seeing/experiencing things! And all those lingering shots of things like knives, guns and chainsaws. The movie is winking at us a bit, because we know those things will be used against all too tender flesh later on.

And if the characters are a bit too flat, a bit too broad? It's okay - at least I can tell them apart, as opposed to some recent horror films. And Jane Levy as Mia is pretty good, if a little annoying - although I think that's intentional. The group as a whole makes really stupid decisions, but hey, it's a rare horror movie that has protagonists who don't. Yes, I wanted to slap Eric when he unwraps the book and then punch him when he reads aloud from the bits that someone has specifically scribbled over with the warning "DO NOT READ," but maybe the mere presence of the book drops your IQ sharply. It would explain a lot.

And when things get cranking the movie ratchets up the terror and gore factor to eleven. This is the goriest feature film I've seen in a long time. These characters get put through the meatgrinder (not literally, but that's about the only thing that doesn't get used). I could have done without the tree rape scene, but it's so iconic in the original that I get that they pretty much HAD to include it, and it's slightly less exploitative than in the original.

About two thirds of the way through the film they start dropping lines and more direct references to the previous film and I'm suddenly annoyed again. I mean, they've been referring to the original the whole time, really, and it was fine. It just seemed like suddenly they were jamming references in, whether they fit or not. The line "her eyes, what happened to her eyes?" is just thrown away, for instance. I liked it better when the references were slightly more oblique. The appearance of the chainsaw was fun and I liked the flooded road, even if the rain seemed more plot driven than realistic.

Things go completely off the rails towards the end, with the blood rain finale making no sense to me, at least not by the rules that are set out by the film itself. By my count the demon only gets three of the required five souls - you can stretch it to four if you count Mia, even though she gets freed. Given that a soul is freed - purified - by fire, then David's death can't count, right? Either way, the finale confrontation between Mia and the summoned Abomination is fun, but ultimately disappointing - the creature effect isn't particularly interesting (where are my Deadites?) and it is way too easily defeated for something that requires such a complicated series of events to be summoned.

The Bottom Line

I'm concentrating on the things that bug me about *Evil Dead*, and that does the film a disservice. It's a good movie, really, a fairly well made horror flick with some great atmosphere, cinematography, pacing and - especially - practical special effects. If I'm disappointed it's because it's so close to being a fantastic film and instead falls a little short. It doesn't fail the first film, exactly, but it certainly isn't as interesting or iconic, but of course that was an awful high bar to try and reach.

70'S CREATURE DOUBLE FEATURE

I'm bundling these two films together for my traditional 70's Creature Feature weekend. In the past I've watched films like *Frogs*, *Piranha*, *Kingdom of the Spiders* and *Prophecy*. I was originally thinking of watching *Squirm* as part of this, but the synergy of the two titles - **Night** *of the Lepus* and **Day** *of the Animals* - won me over. (Only watching one per day this weekend, though, raking and bagging 20 bags of leaves ate into my movie time.)

I've actually seen *Day* before. It was a staple of late 70's/early 80's late night TV. *Night* is new to me, though it's been on my 'must watch' list for a while. Any movie that has giant rabbits as the antagonist has got to have something going for it, right? Right?

The Medium
I actually paid for *Night of the Lepus* (in more ways than one). I rented it on Amazon streaming and that's three bucks I'll never get back. *Day of the Animals* was recently released on Blu-ray, but I'm never going to pay $20 for a William Girdler film. I would have rented it on streaming, but it's not available there either. I ended up watching it on YouTube in a pan-and-scan version. As it approximates how I saw it on TV way back when, I didn't mind. I'm sure the picture quality is fantastic on Blu-ray, but if I want to watch dodgy bird attacks in high-def I'll watch *The Birds*.

NIGHT OF THE LEPUS
"There is a herd of killer rabbits headed this way and we

desperately need your help!"

Director: William F. Claxton, Producer: A. C. Lyles, Written by: Don Holliday,
Gene R. Kearney, Starring: Stuart Whitman, Janet Leigh, Rory Calhoun,
DeForest Kelley

Night of the Lepus is terrible, really. It's poorly shot, written, acted and edited. The special effects are, well, decidedly not special. Other than a few moments - distinguished primarily by a guy in a bunny suit - it's not even in 'so bad it's good' territory. I had a hard time not falling asleep during the film, and was primarily sustained by the occasional bunny attack and those aforementioned 'guy in a suit' moments.

The setup involves a rabbit being dosed with hormones to try and control overpopulation on a desert ranch. It gets released accidentally and soon - giant rabbits! They kill an old prospector - maybe he was dressed as a carrot - which leads to the rancher and some officials dynamiting their burrow. Of course they're rabbits, so they dig their way out and go on a slow motion rampage across indifferently constructed miniature sets before finally being massacred by guns and an electrified train track.

It's possible that this film could be fun with the right group of people. It's completely ridiculous, but played absolutely straight by the actors and director. The rabbits themselves are the most un-menacing group of lethargic bunnies you could think of and even when covered in blood or foaming at the mouth just look cute. Some of the interior sets are okay - and it's fun to see a herd of rabbits hopping in slow motion down the miniature streets of a small town - but in general not a lot of consistency has gone into the effects. Sometimes the rabbits are 'as big as wolves' and sometimes they're as big as elephants.

The 'best' parts are those in which a rabbit attacks an individual, because it's obviously a guy in a bunny suit. It's not even hidden particularly well.

I say that the acting is bad, but it's not really atrocious, at least from the leads. They just seem tone-deaf to the kind of movie they're in. It's not a western, despite appearances. Rory Calhoun in particular seems a little lost dealing with giant bunnies. As for DeForest Kelley, you would think after the first few times he appears I'd stop thinking "Hey, it's Dr. McCoy from *Star Trek*!" You would be wrong.

DAY OF THE ANIMALS

"God sent a plague down on us because we're just a bunch of no-good fellas."

Director: William Girdler, Producer: Edward L. Montoro, Written by: William W. Norton, Eleanor E. Norton, Starring: Christopher George, Leslie Nielsen, Lynda Day George

Day of the Animals is a much better film. Not to say that it's a 'good' film in any traditional sense, but it's more fun and interesting than *Night of the Lepus* - for particular values of 'fun' and 'interesting.'

Day follows a group of back-country hikers as they head out to enjoy a week in the woods. Unfortunately for them, the ozone layer has been depleted to such a significant degree that ultraviolet radiation is turning the animals crazy. Within a couple of days some of them are dead and anyplace above five thousand feet is under assault be animals - bears, mountain lions, snakes, dogs and a whole lot of birds.

Actually, the birds seem to be in charge in this movie. Nominally animals going crazy should result in a frenzy of animals attacking each other, but they all seem to know that it's Man that needs to be attacked. The birds always seem to be present and coordinating things.

The characters are extremely broadly drawn and thin. There's the out-of-place single mother and her son, the young couple, the older couple having marital troubles, the jackass ad-exec, a professor, a news woman, an ill ex-football player, and the obligatory Native American Who Senses Something Is Wrong. They're led by Steve Buckner (Christopher George), a man's-man who knows the back country well and runs these excursions for city folks who want to get away from it all. That's pretty much all you get, and all you need to know.

After the folks head up the mountain there's a scene in the local town diner where we get some exposition about the ozone layer. Things are pretty relaxed in this town. Relaxed enough that the sheriff and his deputies can indulge in a beer, some chili fries and a game of poker during the work day. Menacing music plays when the sheriff orders dessert. "Damn, the sheriff ordered pineapple pie - with ICE CREAM. Shit is getting real."

That night, a wolf attacks the hiker's camp. Even with the buildup, the wolf attack is startling and effective. Don't get used to it, though.

The next day Buckner decides to send the woman who was attacked and her estranged husband up the mountain to a ranger station. While it's actually refreshing for there to be no "We should all head back." "Hell No! I paid good money for this trip!" scene, it still seems a little irresponsible. I mean, we're talking days of travel for an injured woman.

This movie should be called *Leslie Nielsen, Super-Asshole*, by the way. His character is pretty much a jackass all the time.

The husband and wife are attacked almost immediately. "MAN-DEEE!!!!" There's a pretty awesome bird attack, but the blue screen fall off the cliff, not so much.

Back down in the town the sheriff is awoken by a deputy telling him that the military is taking over and evacuating the town, as animals are attacking all over. The sheriff responds by getting a snack. "I'll get in to the office to deal with martial law - right after I have myself a piece o' this here chicken..." He's attacked by rats, but eventually makes it into town to help with the evacuation. Evacuation looks a lot more realistic than in *Night of the Lepus.*

Up on the mountain the group is attacked by mountain lions and separates into reasonable people and jackass followers. Those following Nielsen's character, Jensen, head up the mountain - further into the danger zone - to try and reach the same ranger station that the married couple tried earlier. Jensen, affected by the same radiation, makes the leap from 'asshole' to 'psychopath' really fast - murdering the young husband and trying to rape his wife. Then he decides he's gonna wrestle a bear. Things go well. For the bear.

Girdler tries to cover up how lame the animal attacks are with lots of noise and quick cuts, but it doesn't really help. And if the sun is what's causing the animals to go crazy, why do they almost always attack at night?

The estranged husband from the older couple somehow makes it down to town with a little girl he's rescued earlier. They're set upon by snakes and dogs. When the first truck they get into doesn't start he tries to get to his own car, which is jammed full of rattlesnakes. The lesson is, "Never try."

After that it's all dog attacks down the line, as if they'd run out of money for the other animal trainers. There are a lot of German Shepherds. And dog punching. I've never seen so much dog punching in my life.

And then it's over, just like that. All the affected animals die. The sun returns to normal. It's a bit anti-climactic, but still better than the ending of *Night of the Lepus*.

The Bottom Line

Night of the Lepus was excruciating to watch, but I kind of enjoyed *Day of the Animals*. I'm not sure if it's the gleeful level of cheese or if it was just so much better in comparison. (In fact, you could say it's like Night and Day. I'm sorry, I'l get my coat.) If you can only watch one, make sure it's *Leslie Nielsen, Super Asshole* - you'll be happier for it.

DEEP RISING

"This is turning out to be one hell of a day."

Director: Stephen Sommers, Producers: John Baldecchi, Mario Iscovich, Laurence Mark, Written by: Stephen Sommers, Starring: Treat Williams, Famke Janssen, Anthony Heald, Kevin J. O'Connor, Wes Studi

Look, I like *Deep Rising*, okay. I've admitted it. That's the first step, right?

Deep Rising should really be called *Deep Cheese*, or maybe *Cheap Cthulhu*. It's a low budget monster movie in a decade that really didn't do low budget monster movies very well. You've got *Mimic* - which is halfway decent. *Relic*, which is also fairly decent - until the monster arrives. Does *Anaconda* count? I think so. *Godzilla*... Let's not count *Godzilla*. No, that's being mean, let's count *Godzilla*. Really, the only monster flick in the 1990's that didn't come with a lot of caveats was *Tremors*, right? *Deep Rising* is at least as good as *Relic*. And I had a heckuva lot more fun watching it.

The Medium

I have *Deep Rising* on Blu-ray. Look, the DVD is out of print, alright? And it was a double disk that also includes *The Puppet Masters*, so...

That doesn't make it any better, does it? It was $4.97, does that help?

There's no reason for *Deep Rising* to be on Blu-ray - certainly the picture quality isn't that great and there are no extras (beyond the trailer). It's probably marginally better than an upscaled DVD would be.

The Movie

Deep Rising is an unapologetic B Movie. There's no meta awareness, really, none of the self-referential dialogue that seemed to infest 90's horror films after *Scream*. There's a monster, there's a hero, there's a damsel, there's bad guys, there's comic relief, there's explosions and gunfire and a lot of running.

I think Roger Ebert called this movie a cheap knockoff of *Aliens*, except on a boat. I think it's actually a throwback to a much older sort of monster flick. It's really an adventure movie, more like *King Kong* than *Aliens*. Treat Williams even looks a lot like those square-jawed heroes of the old black and white monster films, like James Franciscus in *The Valley of Gwanji*.

The basic setup: John Finnegan (Williams) is transporting a group of mercenaries across the South China Sea. They're rendezvousing with... something. He doesn't ask questions. His crew, Joey (Kevin O'Connor) and Leila (Una Damon), are a little more nosey and find out that the mercs have brought torpedoes on board. Meanwhile, a huge ocean liner, the *Argonautica*, is on its maiden voyage. Somebody sabotages the navigation and communications and then something attacks the ship from below. When Finnegan and the mercs arrive the ship at first appears deserted, but there are survivors. And of course there's what they're survivors OF.

Everyone is introduced in typical action movie style, with some kind of unique quirk that's supposed to suffice for character development. There's the sex fiend, the Aussie with a chip on his shoulder, the tech guy, the African badass and so on. They're caricatures, but it's a monster movie and they're all going to be eaten anyway, so why get attached? There's a little more given to the 'good guys' - Finnegan is the Crook With a Good Heart, very much in the same mold as Mal in *Firefly*. Joey is the Motormouth Mechanical Genius. We've also got Famke Janssen as a high-class thief and Anthony Heald as a slimy businessman, but there's really not a lot of room for them to stretch - there's way too much running for that.

The monster design is fairly cool, seemingly based off a bobbit worm (Google it if you feel like giving yourself nightmares.) The creature is all tentacles with hooks and multiple fanged mouths for most of it, but there's a huge thing that shows up near the end that's either part octopus or Cthulhu. The biggest drawback is that it's early-days CGI, so it's a bit dodgy at times and too smooth and shiny. (Still better than *Relic*, though.) Other effects, including a poor, half-digested mercenary, fare better and the gore factor is decent, though the blood and guts are more sticky and pink than slick and red.

Things go pear shaped pretty quickly once our heroes arrive and there's a substantial amount of running, shooting and screaming. Parts of the film resemble disaster movies, including a bit where the survivors have to traverse a sunken corridor to get to safety. (Spoiler - they don't all make it.)

I like the humor of the film quite a bit, but it's one of those things that could make or break it for you. Kevin O'Connor makes the best of the gags he's given and his resigned way of admitting how stupid they are is sort of endearing. One of my favorite bits involves a merc who's already being partly eaten by the creature. He gestures to Joey to give him a gun that Joey has and Joey, realizing that eating a bullet would be more merciful than being eaten alive, gives it to him. And then the merc shoots at Joey! Joey screams "Asshole!" as he runs. The merc shrugs, then puts the gun to his temple - but that was the last bullet. Serves him right.

The ending of the film is the best part, though (no, not in the same way as hitting yourself with a hammer). The survivors find themselves on an island. So far so good. Then a roar erupts from the jungle and the camera pans back to give us a shot of your typical Monster Island setup with a volcano erupting in the background and some huge - thing - tearing up trees by the roots as it makes its way to the beach and our heroes.

The Bottom Line

There's not a lot of real quality meat in *Deep Rising* - it's all Grade-Z, mostly circus animals, some filler. It's horror movie junk food, but sometimes that's what you crave and a good steak-and-cheese (hold the steak) can be just as satisfying as a filet mignon if you're in the right mood.

I would totally have gone to see a sequel.

[REC]

"We have to tape everything, Pablo."

*Directors: Jaume Balagueró, Paco Plaza, Producer: Julio Fernández,
Written by: Paco Plaza, Luis A. Berdejo, Jaume Balagueró, Starring:
Manuela Velasco, Ferrán Terraza, Jorge-Yamam Serrano, Pablo Rosso,
David Vert.*

[REC] is my favorite found footage horror film and one of my
favorite horror movies of the last ten years.

I saw the US remake, *Quarantine*, first and if you're going to
watch both, I think that's the way to do it. *Quarantine* is almost a
shot-for-shot remake, so watching it after *[REC]* is really a recipe
for disappointment. (I've avoided *Let Me In* for the same reason - I
loved *Let the Right One In* and feel like I'll be disproportionally hard
on the remake.) If you're only going to see one of them, however,
watch *[REC]*. *Quarantine* is actually a good film, but it has two
problems that *[REC]* does not - first, it uses recognizable actors,
which is always a bit of a kiss of death in a film that's trading on
being 'realistic,' and second, the poster (and cover of the DVD) is
literally the last shot of the movie. There are spoilers and then there
are big middle fingers to the viewer and *Quarantine*'s cover crosses
the line for me.

As of this review I've seen *[REC]2*, but not *[REC]3* (a final entry,
[REC]4: Apocalypse is supposed to be released this year). I liked *2*, but
not as much as the first film. The need to expand and explain always
reduces the horror a bit, for me anyway. I like Michael Myers better
when he was The Shape, not Laurie Strode's older brother.

The Medium

I finally found a copy of *[REC]* at my local video/music/game store (Bullmoose.com, they're awesome) just last week. I've been looking for a while, but there just don't seem to be a lot of copies in circulation, at least not in Maine. There doesn't appear to be a Region A Blu-ray release, but I'm not sure the film needs one - low quality shaky-cam footage is the rule here, and looks just fine in 480p. I do wish there were more extras beyond a short "Making Of" documentary, though.

(*Note: Shout Factory released a Blu-ray collection of all 4 [REC] films in September, 2018.*)

The Movie

The setup to justify the found footage aspect of *[REC]* is that it's being shot by the crew of a local TV station, producing a segment for a show called *While You're Sleeping*. It's just two people, Angela (Manuela Velasco), the reporter, and Pablo (Pablo Rosso), her cameraman. The segment is about life at a local fire station and Angela and Pablo ride along with two firemen - Manu and Alex - to a call about a woman trapped in her apartment.

The genius bit of casting here is that Manuela Velasco is actually a TV personality in Spain. Not that it has the same effect for me, but it must have added an additional layer of verisimilitude when it was released in Spain. Even without that cultural knowledge Velasco is very believable in her role and the 'behind-the-scenes' sequences - as she and her cameraman look for interesting shots and worry about which side to stand on in interviews - really give the proceedings that frisson of realism you hope for in a found footage film.

At the apartment building the crew and the firefighters join two cops who were called as well. Investigating the apartment they find an older woman in nightclothes who is also pretty bloody. She sways and mutters and then, without warning, attacks one of the cops - biting him severely. Alex restrains the woman while everyone else hurries downstairs to try and get the cop outside to an ambulance. Pushing through the group of tenants that are gathered in the lobby they quickly find that the building is being sealed off by the authorities.

I love this building, by the way. I love the winding staircase, the huge doors, the long, narrow halls, the tall windows. I love the mix of residences and businesses. It's just such a cool location. You only get to see it in bits and pieces, which has the effect of making it feel like a maze, like you're never sure where exactly you are.

Just as people are starting to freak out over being sealed in a body falls through the stairwell into the lobby. It's Alex, who is both bitten and severely injured from the fall. This moment is pretty startling, in some ways even worse than the attack by the woman upstairs, because it's just so unexpected. People are shouting, arguing and then - *BAM* - Alex falls to the floor in the background. Jumped the hell out of me the first time.

The film crew, Manu, and the second policeman rush upstairs where they're attacked by the woman again and the policeman is forced to shoot her. The sound of the gunshot in the narrow space is just deafening, like an explosion. The sound editing in general is top-notch throughout the whole film.

It transpires that there's some kind of infection in the building and the authorities have quarantined the entire place until they figure out what to do. Eventually they send in an inspector in hazmat equipment who examines the wounded - Alex and the first policeman. The authorities throughout the film are annoyed and distrustful of the camera crew and Angela and Pablo are, for their part, kind of intrusive. All in the name of journalism, of course. Thankfully not a lot of time is spent defending their right to film or waxing over some journalism award.

When things start to go bad (well, worse), they go bad very fast. There's some handwavium explanation about the infection going slower or faster depending on your blood type, but after a certain point it appears that everyone has the "infected and attacking in 30 seconds" bloodtype. It didn't really bother me during the film, though - in fact, it ratchets the tension up significantly.

One of my favorite sequences actually requires the speedy infection: when Pablo, Angela, and Manu have to descend to the lobby to find the address (by checking mailboxes) of the man who has the keys to the building, they pass the chewed body of a woman. This is a mother who was bit earlier and was handcuffed to the staircase railing as a precaution. When a group of infected broke into the lobby everyone ran, but she was left behind and attacked and partially eaten. The group finds the mailbox and turns back to the stairs - and the woman is standing there, waiting. It's only been a few minutes, but the jump was so much fun I didn't care.

With multiple people infected Pablo and Angela end up having to take refuge in the penthouse, only to find that it is the source of the contagion. The apartment seems to have been set up by an agent of the Vatican who was researching a case of demonic possession. Saying much more would give things away, but it's a very different ending than *Quarantine* - at least as far as the foundations of the infection go. I go back and forth as to which version I prefer, but this time around *[REC]*'s back story won out. It's damn creepy (although I find *Quarantine*'s to be more plausible - and frightening in its own way because of that).

I'm pretty happy with the quality of the found footage aspect. Yeah, things are perhaps a bit more centered and steady than might be realistic if the camera was held by an amateur, but Pablo is a professional cameraman, so I buy it. And it's not like that all the time - there are points where the camera is turned on and not pointing at anything, there are moments of shaky running cam that are so bad I almost got nausea. Night vision is used sparingly and to great effect and only when they finally lose the use of the main spotlight. (Which is actually smashed instead of falling prey to 'plot-required' mechanical difficulties.')

The last ten minutes or so are edge-of-your-seat tense. I've seen it before and I still caught myself holding my breath at certain points.

The Bottom Line

[REC] is just an awesome horror movie and the peak of the found footage genre. There are a few pieces of plot that don't make a lot of sense and some of the camerawork is, perhaps, a little too good, but it works so well as a whole that I don't really mind. The sequel is also good, though not quite to the same level as the first.

THE VISITOR (1979)

"Mommy, mommy, mommy, look!"

Director: Giulio Paradisi, Producer: Ovidio G. Assonitis, Written by: Luciano Comici, Robert Mundi, Story by: Giulio Paradisi, Ovidio G. Assonitis, Starring: Paige Conner, Joanne Nail, John Huston, Lance Henriksen, Shelley Winters.

If I had remembered that I had already seen *The Visitor* I wouldn't have bought the damn thing.

It's not that it's completely worthless, far from it. It's got some interesting visuals and ideas swimming around in all that craziness - it's just not something I feel like I need to own. I guess that's the lesson I take away - don't buy something unless you're sure you seen it or not. Also, they had projector TVs in 1979, which is something I didn't know.

Also, WTF? This film is crazy! Not Nobuhiko Obayashi *House* crazy, but still pretty messed up. It's as if Lucio Fulci got tapped to direct an *Omen* ripoff as produced by Irwin Allen. It's a 'devil' movie, but with aliens instead of God and Satan. It's got Shirley Winters singing "Shortnin' Bread" while dressed as Mary Poppins. It's got Django as Jesus - at least I think he's Jesus. He could be my friend Greg Hyland, though, as they look(ed) pretty similar.

The Medium
I bought the Blu-ray used in a horror-movie binge over the summer. It's perfectly serviceable, but there's still plenty of noise, scratches and film damage. The cover is reversible, which I guess is nice. There are a handful of extras, including a fun interview with Lance Henriksen.

The Movie

After a bizarre opening sequence in which John Huston stands around in a desert while a little girl gets hit in the face with potato shavings, we get a rundown of how things stand as delivered by Jesus to a group of bald kids. No I'm not kidding. I think that opening sequence (which is pretty interesting, visually) is supposed to represent a cosmic struggle between the forces of good and evil. I think.

The basic point that Django... er, Jesus, is trying to get across is that there was a super-evil bad guy (Sateen - get it?) that was defeated by a super-awesome good guy and an army of birds, but not before passing his evil on by doing the nasty with women on earth. So his evil is like a genetic trait that gets passed down and occasionally expresses itself in evil offspring with magic powers, and then someone calls cosmic 911 and super-awesome good guy (the eponymous Visitor, played by John Huston) goes and does something about it. The Visitor shows up and says they've got a new sighting - it's an eight year old girl in Atlanta, Georgia.

The girl, Katy, is manifesting powers, including telekinesis and the ability to swear like a sailor. She blows up a basketball player with her mind, I think. I dunno. Her mom is a nice but bland person who is being wooed by the basketball team owner who is beholden to a weird cabal that seems to want her to have more kids. More kids like Katy.

Much of the movie revolves around Katy being a dick. She 'accidentally' paralyzes her mother, Barbara, when one of her birthday presents turns out to be a handgun. She torments some boys at a skating rink, eventually throwing a couple of them out of the rink. The detective that is investigating the shooting (Glenn Ford) gets murdered by her pet hawk. She swears at everyone, including the housekeeper who, to be fair, does slap her an awful lot. (I THINK housekeeper is supposed to be there to guard the mother, but she's spectacularly useless at that. And she's mean enough to Katy that you're expecting some kind of retaliation, but she's left alone.)

When Huston shows up to confront her (and get his ass handed to him at Pong) you wonder if there's going to be some epic confrontation of psychic powers between them, but there isn't. Even later, when Katy does try to kill him, it's mostly Scooby-doo running between doorways and one loose screw on a fire escape.

There are abductions, attempted murders, weird looking houses and one epic bird attack, but there's not a lot of sense to be had. Sometimes John Huston goes to a rooftop and holds his hands up while lights appear. Sometimes Katy does gymnastics. The hawk attacks people. Sam Peckinpah shows up for four minutes and Mel Ferrer menaces in a distinguished way. It sometimes makes sense and sometimes doesn't. The end made me think Neo was going to appear and bend spoons.

So much of the film feels like a low-budget Italian exploitation flick - the nonsense plot, the occasionally amazing visual set pieces, the over-the-top score. And then there's Shelly Winters slapping a kid and it's all 'you got your peanut butter in my wasabi peas,' two great tastes that are WTF together.

The Bottom Line

The Visitor is a bizarre and nonsensical film that's occasionally visually arresting. It's packed with top-flight 70's actors in weird roles. It's an experience, but your enjoyment may vary significantly from scene to scene. and you may end up questioning whether it's an experience that you needed to have.

THE LAST MAN ON EARTH

"I can't live a heartbeat away from hell – and forget it."

*Directors: Sidney Salkow, Ubaldo B. Ragona, Producer: Robert L. Lippert,
Written by: Logan Swanson, William F. Leicester, Starring: Vincent Price,
Franca Bettoia, Giacomo Rossi Stuart.*

I read Richard Matheson's *I Am Legend* pretty late in my sci-fi reading history. I'd already seen and read a dozen things that were inspired by (or blatantly ripped off) the book, but it still had power, and is well worth a read if you get a chance.

While you can see its influence in things like the original *Night of the Living Dead* I don't think anyone's really done the original story justice - official adaptations included. *Omega Man* has its own cheesy glories, but as an adaptation of the novel it fails miserably. *I Am Legend* was a fun movie - and in some ways captured a bit of that epic loneliness of the main character - but it's an action movie at the end of the day, more concerned with the CGI monsters and action set pieces.

No, *The Last Man on Earth* - despite the slow pacing, bad acting (except for Price) and the low-budget feel to the whole affair - is the most faithful. Whether that's a good thing or not is a matter of opinion. I happen to think it's the best of the bunch, with the changes from the novel being necessary (especially the ending).

The Medium

For years all I've had was a DVD copy that was a part of one of those '50 Horror Classics' type collections. It's pretty crappy, cropped on the sides and with significant dust/scratches/damage. Luckily, Scream Factory has released a Blu-ray version as part of its *Vincent Price Collection II*. I don't own the set yet, but it's something I hope to pick up eventually.

The picture is a revelation compared to the low-quality versions I've seen on TV and DVD. The picture is sharp and detailed and the contrast is much improved, providing a depth sorely lacking in previous releases.

The Movie

It's the end of the world and we know it. The sun rises on an empty LA. Bodies and debris litter the streets. In a residential neighborhood, in a house festooned with garlic and mirrors, the Last Man on Earth is waking up.

The bleakness of Morgan's existence is made obvious early on in *The Last Man on Earth*. The shots of various parts of LA with corpses strewn about, empty streets, debris everywhere. Then there's Morgan's house - full of just the most essential things, piled up on every surface. His living room includes a record player, but it also has a shortwave radio setup and a lathe where he makes stakes. There are what look like blood splatters on the walls. This is a man who is just surviving, and really, if you're the last person on earth who do you have to clean up for?

Normally I dislike narration, but I'll make an exception for Vincent Price. It's really a one-man show, this movie, and he does a fantastic job - alternately stoic and on the edge of breaking down.

It's an average day for Morgan, bleak as it is. Need garlic and gas. Load the corpses he finds outside of his house into the back of his station wagon and drive them to a smoking pit where he dumps the bodies. Then it's a trip to the grocery store, past piles of corpses.

At this point the rational part of your brain has questions. Generators still working, gas still available after three years? Food still neatly stacked on shelves? Corpses EVERYWHERE? In a modern movie all this stuff would be smashed, the food taken during the collapse of society, but it was a different time.

A good portion of Morgan's day is going door to door, room to room, killing what can only be described as vampires. It's gotta be vampires, right? We've got garlic, mirrors, and stakes. Yet they look and act more like zombies. Especially once he returns home just before sundown and the creatures come out of the dark to assault his house.

That look on his face as they assault the house. Imagine three years of that. Gah.

The next day Morgan goes to visit his wife's crypt. One eerie detail: the cemetery is jammed with the rows of cheap, makeshift crosses. He falls asleep and by the time he wakes up the sun has already set. He's forced to run a gauntlet of the creatures to get to his car and back to the house.

Dude. They're zombies. Slow-moving, fairly weak, trouble in groups. Zombies.

This must have been one of the first post-apocalyptic movies that had all these elements. A wrecked city, a lone survivor watching films of his family, checking on the radio for survivors, slowly going mad. Vincent Price is really good in this. I mean he's good normally, but just really understated and effective here.

We eventually get a flashback to life before, when the plague was just getting started, and geez, that's an effective flashback. Here's what life was like before your daughter was taken away to be burned by the military. Before your wife came back from the grave to try and kill you. And your former best friend is now the monster trying to kill you every night. We get a very good sense of how things are falling apart. And they actually use the word "vampires."

Unfortunately, nobody is a good actor in this film so far except Price. It's not horrible, as most of the film is just him, but it's noticeable when any other actors have lines.

There's a bit in the flashback where the military has come and taken his daughter, who has been infected. He rushes to the pit where they're burning bodies, the same pit he's dumping at in the earlier part of the film. The military won't let him in and he wails that it's his daughter in there. The soldier's reply: "Mister, a lot of daughters are in there. Including my own."

That is some dark shit right there.

You know, it's small bits that stick out to me. That he doesn't clean up the sawdust from making stakes. The joy on Morgan's face when he sees the stray dog. The horror at the return of his wife. It's awesome - awful, but awesome.

Eventually Morgan finds someone else IS alive. A woman named Ruth that runs when she first sees him, though he's able to catch up to her and convince her to come with him. What's interesting (at least to me) is that he's less overjoyed at finding her than he was at finding the dog. Maybe it's the suspicion that things will all go wrong. He's right about that, and Ruth is hiding a terrible secret. One that will eventually lead to Morgan's death.

The ending is substantially different from the book, but it *is* more exciting, with a chase, a gunfight and a final confrontation in a church. There's some dialogue with Ruth about him being just as much a monster to those he's killed as they are to him, but it gets a bit muddled in the rush. (And I wish he'd called them monsters instead of 'freaks' for some reason.) There's no real representation of a new order taking the place of the old, it's just a bunch of people in black rushing about with guns, suddenly.

The Bottom Line

It's definitely a low-budget movie, but *The Last Man on Earth* is a lot better than I remember it being. There's some care and thought put into the piece and I appreciated those a lot more this time around. Vincent Price is great and if the rest of the cast doesn't measure up, well, who does? Like the other adaptations of *I Am Legend* this one is flawed, but even a flawed gem shines if you tilt it just right to the light.

THE LAST WINTER

"We shouldn't be here."

Director: Larry Fessenden, Producers: Larry Fessenden, Jeffrey Levy-Hinte,
Written by: Larry Fessenden, Robert Leaver, Starring: Ron Perlman, Pato
Hoffmann, James LeGros, Connie Britton.

This is a holdover from the last time we had a DVD subscription
on Netflix. I was supposed to get *A Cat in the Brain*, a 1990 Lucio
Fulci film, but that's on a short wait so they sent this film, which has
likely been sitting in my DVD queue since it came out.

It was probably the setting that drew me. I'm a sucker for horror
movies that are set in the arctic/antarctic or even just during winter.
Not sure why - something to do with the alien look and feel to the
settings, maybe. Or perhaps it's just that, regardless of what monster
or villain is trying to kill the protagonists, mother nature is also
waiting her turn to get a knife in.

That Ron Perlman is in it was also a plus. Connie Britton. I like
Kevin Corrigan, though it sometimes seems like he's the poor man's
Mark Ruffalo.

I dunno. I think I'd read Dan Simmons' *The Terror* about the time
this came out, so that might have had something to do with it as
well. I'm not even sure why I'm trying to track down why I added it
to my list.

The Medium

DVD from Netflix. Serviceable, but not great. Some extras,
including a commentary track. I listened to that a bit, looking for
some info on the ending, but it's a bit pompous and boring - at least

the section I listened to.

The Movie

The Last Winter is set at some point in the very near future. An oil company has managed to get permission to start a preliminary drilling site in the Arctic National Wildlife Refuge. The primary setting is a small outpost where the lead team is doing prep work and an impact study. Ed Pollack (Perman) arrives to get things moving so that drilling equipment can come in and they can get started, but things aren't quite right. It's too warm, for one thing. Too warm for the ice roads to be laid down. Hoffman, the lead climate scientist, says that even the permafrost is melting. Ed isn't willing to take no for an answer, though, regardless of what dangers may arise from the warming ice.

So, decent setup. Your typical isolated base, only reachable by plane. Full of characters broadly drawn and conflicts... also broadly drawn. Hoffman and Pollack are, of course, antagonists. The Company vs the Scientist. (That Hoffman is sleeping with the project head, Abby Sellers (Britton), who once had a relationship with Pollack, just adds more friction.) There's obviously something effecting the youngest member of the crew, Maxwell (Zach Gifford), who keeps asking about the capped test well the company made to prove there was oil to be had.

There's an art-film feel to things. The music is slow and mostly piano, with a limited number of themes. There's a lot of slow, sweeping pans of desolate arctic landscape that end with the face of someone staring meaningfully into the distance. The director likes to do long, handheld shots following characters in the tight confines of the base (which is really just a bunch of trailers welded together). It's a little flat, a little pat, but there's some gold to be mined out of a climate change horror movie that isn't focused on tornadoes with sharks in them.

Unfortunately, this movie is unfocused and vague. Interesting things are brought up and never fully explored. Maxwell seems to think the capped well is haunted or something, but nothing comes of that. Ravens show up as, maybe, harbingers of something old that's being released from the ice, but they're never used as anything more than set dressing. Maxwell disappears for most of a day and when he returns one of the characters remarks that according to something on his suit (GPS maybe?) he travelled three hundred miles. Everybody looks around meaningfully, but nothing is ever done with that either.

Weird events start to pile up. It rains in the middle of the arctic winter. Wind storms appear inside research shelters, but not outside. The tracks of a herd of caribou appear from nowhere and go nowhere. A team member has a nose bleed that will not stop. Maxwell disappears and on a video tape he's left behind some - thing - appears to carry him off. (Nobody reacts to this except Hoffman, so maybe it's supposed to be a hallucination.) Hoffman opines that maybe hydrogen sulfide is seeping out of the ground, causing everyone to have mental issues.

In a briefly glimpsed log entry Hoffman seems to suggest that they've reached a point of runaway climate change. "The Last Winter" may be upon them.

Deaths pile up. A plane crashes into the camp. Hoffman and Pollack make a last-ditch journey to find help, but there's something out there in the wastes with them. The spirits of those long dead animals whose corpses make up the oil Pollack is so desperate to get out of the ground? The Wendigo? It's left open for us to decide what really happens. Even a coda with Britton's character in which she wakes up in an abandoned hospital and steps out into a rain soaked parking lot doesn't show or give us an answers.

To be honest, by then I didn't give a shit. There are a lot of ominous things said in *The Last Winter*, however it's all presented in such a disjointed fashion that you get the feeling that there's no real coherent vision. That the writer just threw a bunch of terms together and thought they sounded cool.

The whole film is inconsistent. You'll have beautifully framed and photographed shots of desolate landscape and they'll be followed by poorly framed/focused/lit shots of main character interactions. Some of it feels like they gave a camera to a grip and said "you're second unit, give me shots of the kitchen." The acting is low key - too much so. When behavior differences show up they're abrupt and seem to have no organic evolution. People are fine. Then they're crazy. The eerie moments - and there are a few - are placed with little regard to pace or timing. There's really only one good scare, and it should have been followed up on, but is - as a lot of things are in the film - abandoned. As slow as the film is it also feels like it was created by someone with ADD, jumping from one 'cool' idea to the next without building a coherent mood or theme.

The Bottom Line

I really wanted to like *The Last Winter*. It's got some great actors, some good ideas and the occasional eerie moment. Unfortunately the uneven quality just left me feeling annoyed and disappointed. There's a good movie in here somewhere, but I just didn't have the patience to find it. In the end the movie is as ponderous and yet insubstantial as its monster.

ARGENTO/FULCI FILMS I HAVEN'T SEEN DOUBLE FEATURE

Lucio Fulci and Dario Argento are two of my favorite Italian horror movie directors, so it's a little weird that I haven't seen all of their films yet. I'll probably never see all of Fulci's work, as he had a long career with comedies, westerns and (gasp!) family films before jumping into giallos and horror. I may eventually see all of Argento's films, though - even if I've held off watching much of anything post-*Opera*. The gaps do mean I have a decent chance of watching a film from one or the other that I haven't seen in any given October. For this theme weekend I randomly ended up with two films that were towards the end of one director's career and near the beginning of the other.

A CAT IN THE BRAIN
(AKA NIGHTMARE CONCERT)

Director: Lucio Fulci, Producers: Antonio Lucidi, Luigi Nannerini, Written by: Lucio Fulci, Giovanni Simonelli, Antonio Tentori, Starring: Lucio Fulci, Brett Halsey, Jeoffrey Kennedy, Malisa Longo.

A Cat in the Brain is a weird little film, which I know sounds redundant when I'm talking about a Lucio Fulci movie. It's kind of a clip-show - with some of the gorier bits of previous Fulci movies edited in around a framing story about a director that may or may not be going mad. And the director in question is Lucio Fulci, and by that I mean he's playing himself. A simplified highly stylized version of himself, I'm sure, but it makes everything that goes on so much weirder.

I had the film described to me as a proto-meta horror movie, a direct precursor to movies like *Wes Craven's New Nightmare*. A commentary on both horror movies in general and on Fulci horror movies in specific. Of course I also had it described to me as the lazy 'greatest hits' tour of a hack director out of original ideas, so there's that.

Medium

I rented the 2009 DVD from Grindhouse Releasing. Normally this is a 2 DVD set with extras on the second DVD, but I got it from Netflix so it was only the main disk. There are some trailers and a Q&A with Fulci at *Fangoria*'s 1996 Weekend of Horrors. Not sure what's on the second disk, but there's no commentary track on the film itself. The picture is fine for a DVD.

The Movie

There's an opening sequence in which someone - presumably Fulci - sits at a large desk, working on something. The camera descends... and suddenly we're inside his soft, pink, bloody brain. And then a cat starts tearing at it. Two cats, maybe. Tearing with their claws and devouring bits of brain.

Given the context of the rest of the film this is an interesting metaphor for the strange and disturbing ideas and imagery that are the obsession of horror film directors. What kind of brain is it that comes up with things like splinters in eyeballs and feeding people to pigs? A disturbed brain, a brain with some kind of creature pulling and tearing. Geez - I'd hate to see what kind of things are playing with my soft grey matter. Probably spiders.

After that we have some clips from *Touch of Death*, which involves a cannibal. Lots of gory shots of dismemberment. We then see that this is the film Lucio Fulci is working on, and after finishing the last shot (the feeding to pigs scene) he calls for lunch. However when he arrives at the restaurant he can't get past visions of the film - a filet and steak tartar remind him of the awful things he's just shot. He ends up leaving the restaurant and going home.

It seems that the horrific visions he creates in front of the camera are starting to infect his normal life. He starts to have hallucinations in which normal, day-to-day occurrences become terrible recreations of bits of his movies (or new bits - I'll admit to not recognizing every gory moment as being from another film). Worried that he's becoming unstable and losing his grip on reality he goes to a psychiatrist who advises him that he's 'breaking down the barriers between what's real and what you film." Yeah, helpful, thanks Doc.

Pressure mounts on Fulci, as he appears to be filming two movies at once. One of them looks like a soft-core porn movie about Nazis and sadism (*Sodoma's Ghost*, maybe?), and Fulci questions the point of even making these sorts of films anymore. A German film crew arrives to interview him, but an extended hallucination of shooting another Nazi scene occurs and in the aftermath Fulci finds that he's assaulted the film crew.

Fulci doesn't appear to pulling a lot of punches in this film - he's not out to make himself look good. In the hallucination of shooting the Nazi orgy he's presented as both voyeuristic and even fueling the events - licking his lips and urging the actors on to even more degrading acts. That he looks a little like a bumbling professor most of the time makes those moments when he's acting the degenerate all the more disturbing.

Soon his psychiatrist has decided to take advantage of Fulci's problem, hypnotizing the hapless director into thinking that the hallucinations are real and that he's descending into madness, committing horrible murders. Meanwhile, the psychiatrist, Professor Swharz, takes out his rage at his wife's infidelity by murdering prostitutes. This... is all pretty ridiculous. The good doctor looks absurd in a hoody and enormous grin. I think he's supposed to be setting up Fulci to take the fall for these, but it's honestly not very clear (Fulci film - should have expected). He even had an epic villain speech where he announces his intentions and waxes about how stupid it is to blame real-life violence on movies - but it's to an empty room, so kinda wasted.

Fulci's visions get worse and worse. Pretty much every mundane thing - a drink, a microwaved dinner, a local girl in a wheelchair - all turn into visions of some horrific moment from his films. (The film clips are all the gory bits and come frequently - they're all low-budget, but entertaining in their own way. The burnt girl in the wheelchair is particularly creepy, though.) Eventually, convinced that the murders he's seeing on the TV are things he's done, he calls a detective friend, presumably to confess. However, the detective is on vacation so Fulci goes once again to the psychiatrist.

At one point he's driving along and starts chasing a guy who flees directly down the road, of course, never thinking to move off the side into the trees. (I'd give him more crap about that, but I've seen *Prometheus*.) Hilariously, this guy - who seems to be homeless - recognizes the man trying to run him down and yells "What's the matter with you, Fulci?" As if Lucio Fulci is famous enough that random people on the street recognize him. Like if I was walking and Wes Craven tried to run me down. What's your problem, Wes? And then, just when I'm thinking Fulci only wants to get by and to his destination, he runs the homeless guy over. Like four times.

It's a hallucination of course. Most of the film is of poor Fulci reacting to these horrible scenes he's created. There's a lot of subtext about art and whether the man who creates monsters must be a monster himself, but it's all throwaway - more sub-subtext. While Fulci is honestly horrified to see these things outside of their context - the film set - within the film production context he actively seeks out and revels in them. The film crew that he assaults seems to be pleased to have a Fulci story to tell. And the psychiatrist gets to spout all the dialogue about violence and media. Of course the authorities will believe it's Fulci! He makes those horrible movies, after all.

The ending is abrupt and unsatisfying. Fulci faints at a murder scene and when the police arrive the next morning he fumbles to explain - but they've already caught the real killer, who followed Fulci to the park. It's all wrapped up, but Fulci's problems are never really followed up on - maybe because they're struggles he just has to live with. There's a fun little second ending after that, but the plot line - that I really did become involved in - has already ended, and badly.

The Bottom Line

I was surprised at *A Cat in the Brain*. It really is a low-budget clip show. But it's also an interesting and somewhat fun meta-commentary on Fulci's films and being a person associated with creating horror. It's low budget - I mean it's cheap as hell - but strangely endearing. As with all Fulci, enter at your own risk. But it's definitely an worth a watch.

FOUR FLIES ON GREY VELVET

Director: Dario Argento, Producer: Salvatore Argento, Written by: Dario Argento, Luigi Cozzi, Mario Foglietti, Starring: Michael Brandon, Mimsy

Farmer, Jean-Pierre Marielle, Francine Racette, Bud Spencer.

I hadn't even heard of this film until recently. It was apparently released in the US for the first time in 2009, and only sporadically elsewhere in what might have been bootleg versions. It's Argento's third film and is sometimes referenced as the final part of his 'Animal Trilogy' - along with *The Bird With the Crystal Plumage* and *The Cat o' Nine Tails*. (There's really no connection other than the titles, so *Four Flies* can be safely watched without having seen the other films.)

I went into this knowing nothing about it, except that it was an Argento film I hadn't seen. (There are a few, actually, but this was the only one I that was completely new to me.) My enjoyment of the film may be outsized compared to the actual quality (and the quality of later films, like *Deep Red* or *Suspiria*), but that's probably a result of watching it so soon after Fulci's *A Cat in the Brain*. The difference in level of quality and skill was pretty striking.

The Medium

I watched *Four Flies on Grey Velvet* via streaming. The quality was decent, though not HD. It had the '40 missing seconds' added, but in Italian and without subtitles. If the movie is ever released on Blu-ray in the US I'll probably pick it up.

The Movie

Roberto is a drummer in a rock band. (All the music is provided by Enio Morricone and there's prog-rock, jazz and some electronic sounding stuff.) There's a mysterious figure following him around after rehearsals and even during the day. One night he finally confronts the stalker, having followed them to an abandoned theater. The stalker pulls a knife, they struggle and in the melee Roberto stabs the stalker. This is bad enough, but there's also someone else in the theater. Someone wearing a creepy puppet mask who takes pictures of Robert standing over the body, holding the bloody knife. Roberto runs, but is soon contacted by the person who took the pictures. They're not going to the police, no - they want to torment Robert, before killing him.

Man this is a stylish film. I know that's like Argento's thing, but there's some really awesome cinematography and framing in this film. Right off the bat we've got shots from the inside of a guitar, slow spins to reveal people standing outside of windows, and a shot of a fly between two cymbals with the drummer out of focus behind it. It's just so visually interesting compared to Fulci's straightforward compositions.

Also, that puppet mask? That is damn creepy. I kind of wish it had kept appearing throughout the film, but it's not that sort of giallo.

I'm not sure what to make of Roberto. He seems a likeable enough guy, but he's also willing to cover up his involvement in a man's death. He appears to be somewhat distant and isolated, even from his beautiful wife and his band mates. Maybe that's just the stress he's under, but it ended up having the effect of leaving me feeling distanced from him as well.

There's a shot that appears to be a cemetery. Headstones in a white glare, over-exposed. Then the contrast starts to drop, the glare fades... and it's a public square on a middle-eastern country. What we thought were tombstones are actually the curved entrances into the surrounding building. There's a public execution going on and we watch the executioner begin his work. This is a recurring dream that Roberto has and is one of the few potentially supernatural touches in the film - if we take it as a premonition. Though it's just as likely that it's a representation of Roberto's increasing fear and paranoia, mixed with a story told at a party.

The blackmailer invades Roberto's house, leaving pictures of the killing. They even enter at night and almost kill Roberto with a garrote before telling him that they want him to suffer first. At this point I'd be going to the police, murder rap or no, but instead Robert seeks out the advice of God.

I don't generally expect a Dario Argento film to be funny. So when Roberto goes to talk to his friend Godfrey and calls out 'hey God!' and there's a burst of music and a chorus singing 'hallelujah!' I almost snorted my drink. There's a substantial amount of humor in the film, between a bumbling mailman, God and the Professor (two homeless gentlemen), and a gay detective. Whether it works for anyone else or not I actually enjoyed the humor. It's a little jarring, but the scenes - particularly with God and the Professor talking to Roberto at a Funeral Arts convention - are just hilarious to me. (One of the people at the convention tries lying in a coffin only to complain that it's a little too tight. The response of the vendor - "None of our customers have ever come back with a complaint...")

The gay detective is way too over the top, but the actor is so good in the role that I can almost forgive the cartoony nature of the presentation. I found myself wishing the entire movie was about this guy on his quest to finally solve a case. He's only around for a short time, though, and he's sorely missed after an unfortunate meeting with the killer. I was pretty impressed that there was a positively portrayed gay character in a giallo in 1971, even if he's almost a caricature.

There are a number of plot twists and turns of course. This is, after all, an Argento film. Murders are highly stylized affairs with inventive and almost beautiful imagery. A maid out to blackmail the blackmailer is in a park full of people during the day - and then she's suddenly alone at night, locked in with the blackmailer (who quickly becomes a killer). A cousin of Roberto's wife is a suspect - until she too is murdered in spectacular style.

And then... oh dear. The 'last image can be recovered from the victim's eyes' crap. This is why I quit watching *Fringe* the first time it aired. It's still dumb... but it does look kinda cool, with eyeballs, lasers, glass globes, and a blurry image projected on a circular screen.

The end comes quickly after the reveal of the murderer. There's some crappy pop psychology, slow motion bullet time (decades before *The Matrix* - though it's pretty limited), slow motion car crash decapitations and more prog-rock soundtrack music than you can shake a stick at. Does it all make sense? Probably not, though it felt more coherent than some of Argento's films.

The acting is fairly decent, if broad, and I was pleasantly surprised by the dubbing. Mimsy Farmer as Roberto's wife Nina is a standout, as is Jean-Pierre Marielle as the detective Arrosio. The final confrontation was marred by the inclusion of several seconds that had been excluded from previous versions of the film. These are mostly part of a sequence in which the killer explains their actions and are all in Italian with no subtitles. So I was left with the impression that the killer had gone crazy because sometimes they just randomly speak in Italian.

The Bottom Line

Four Flies on Grey Velvet is a really enjoyable giallo with all that entails - including elaborate killings, stylish people and settings, and some convoluted plot twists. It may not represent Argento at the height of his powers, but it's still a pretty entertaining film.

CREEPSHOW

"Just tell it to call you Billie!"

Director: George A. Romero, Producer: Richard P. Rubinstein, Written by: Stephen King, Starring: Hal Holbrook, Adrienne Barbeau, Fritz Weaver, Leslie Nielsen, Ted Danson, Carrie Nye, E. G. Marshall, Viveca Lindfors, Stephen King.

George Romero. Stephen King. EC Comics... well, in spirit, anyway. *Creepshow* was a staple of Halloween in my teens, one of those films that always got rented (if it was available, that is) around the 31st. It has a certain kind of ghoulish glee that I associate with a childhood love of monsters and horror movies. When horror was fun AND creepy. (One of the reasons I love *Trick 'r Treat* is that it seems to embrace that same level of love for Halloween.)

Back in 1982, when *Creepshow* was released, I hadn't actually seen any EC comics. I think they were out of print at the time, or only available via expensive hardcover reprints. Instead I associated the movie with the more palid horror comics that DC put out in the 70's: *The Witching Hour*, *House of Secrets* and *House of Mystery*. I loved those comics - the illustrated equivalent of a fire-side ghost story - and never realized that they were watered down by the Comics Code Authority until much later, when I finally got to see copies of *Tales From the Crypt* and *Vault of Horror*.

At one point I had the comic adaptation, illustrated by Bernie Wrightson, and I just about wore it out reading it. I wish I still had a copy, but it's disappeared in the intervening years - perhaps finally falling apart or maybe just lurking in a comic box in the basement, biding its time until it can lurch forth and... I dunno, give me a paper cut or something.

The Medium

I've got the Warner Brothers DVD release of *Creephsow* which has the widescreen on one side and a full screen version on the other (both written on a tiny black band around the center hole and impossible to read in dim light). The 'special features' are pretty much the trailer. I'm not calling 'interactive menus' and 'scene access' special. From what I understand the US Blu-ray release also only includes the trailer. I'd love to have some commentary, some featurettes on the creature/makeup design, info on the Berni Wrightson comic adaptation... ah well.

(A Shout Factory Blu-ray with a bunch of extras was released in October 2018.)

The Movie

I'm breaking this out by segment.

Prologue

Both the prologue and epilogue feature a boy named Billy and his parents. In the prologue Billy's getting a dressing down by his father for reading horror comics. After a fatherly slap across Billy's face the comics are thrown out. While a self-satisfied dad sits in his easy chair Billy sits upstairs, cursing his father. At the window appears The Creep from his horror comic, beckoning Billy to come closer...

The boy, if I remember correctly, is played by one of Stephen King's sons. Tom Atkins (*The Fog*, *Halloween 3*) is the dad.

"Father's Day"

This starts things of in typical EC comics style, with a wealthy family of degenerates and a dark secret. Every Father's day the Granthams get together to remember their patriarch, a domineering and abusive man named Nathan Grantham. The youngest of the group has a new husband, which conveniently allows for the rest of the family to tell him the tale of Nathan's murder - by his own daughter - many years before.

This is Aunt Bedelia, who arrives late and goes to the old man's grave to drink and curse at him for having her lover killed (the event that precipitated Grantham's murder). She spills her drink on the grave and, seemingly in response, Nathan rises from the ground and sets about killing people and asking - in a literally gravel-filled voice

- for his Father's Day cake.

This is actually my least favorite segment, but it's still loads of fun. Watching Ed Harris be the hick is a hoot, and the maggoty remains of Nathan Grantham are a memorable effect (as is the Father's Day cake he eventually makes for himself). The segment also establishes the visual theme for the entire movie - bright reds and blues with graphic backgrounds reminiscent of EC comics. Transitions and end sequences are often in actual comic book format and some scenes are even shown with a traditional comic book 'gutter' - the white area around each frame.

"The Lonesome Death of Jordy Verril"

A down-on-his-luck farmer sees a meteor crash on his property and goes to investigate. Dreams of selling it to the local college are dashed when he pours cold water on the steaming meteorite, cracking it. He puts the pieces in a bucket - after pouring the glowing contents of the hollow meteorite into the crater - and goes to have a beer and watch wrestling.

Soon he realizes that the fingers he used to touch the meteorite are turning green - growing fuzzy with something plant-like. Over the course of the evening the growth gets worse - everywhere he's touched and been. "Not down there!" Oh yes, down there too. Outside, the cabin is becoming overgrown and plant life spreads in a circle out from the crater.

In a desperate attempt to alleviate the itching Jordy jumps into a tub full of water - but that's just what the green growth wants. In the end Jordy finds a way out, but given the weather report the rest of the world may not be so lucky.

Let's just say up front that acting is not one of Stephen King's strong suits. I've always had a soft spot for this segment, though. Watching it again this time I realized a chapter in my *Monster War* novel - where a lawn comes to life and tries to kill the heroes - is inspired by this segment. I didn't realize it at the time, but it's obvious looking at it now.

"Something to Tide You Over"

This segment could also be called "Leslie Nielsen, Super Asshole" - just like *Day of the Animals*. A wealthy man finds out he's been cuckolded and takes revenge on his wife and her lover by burying them in the sand up to their necks and waiting for the tide to come in. He even watches the whole thing on remote video. Unfortunately for him, they come back. And it doesn't matter how long he can hold his breath.

This one is always a good time. Nielsen is a ham sandwich of crazy, but it's fun to watch. Ted Dansen is more interesting as a water-logged corpse than he is as the lover. The makeup effects are great - particularly the spurt of dark water when the zombies are shot.

"The Crate"

A college custodian finds a crate under the stairs and calls a professor, Dexter Stanley, as it appears to be very old. When the two open the crate a monster inside attacks and kills the custodian. Stanly flees, running into a grad student who also ends up being killed by the monster. Even more distraught, Stanley flees to the house of his friend, fellow professor Henry Northrup.

Northrup, a mild-mannered man who is severely hen-pecked by his wife Billie, sees the crate and the monster as an opportunity to rid himself of his wife for good. He sets about cleaning the mess before luring his wife to the college, where the crate - and the monster - wait.

This has always been my favorite. I just love monster stories, and the thing in the crate is a great monster. Yeah, upon a closer look it's just a monkey with sharp teeth, but damn, it's effective. Hal Holbrook as Henry and Adrienne Barbeau as Wilma "Call me Billie" Northrup are pretty good, but Fritz Weaver is fantastic - one of the few times in a horror movie I've seen an adult male actor appear believably traumatized by the goings on.

Also, is it just me, or is this the basic plot for *Relic*? Just me? Okay then.

"They're Creeping Up on You"

A ruthless businessman, Upson Pratt, who's afraid of germs and bugs spends the night fighting cockroaches in his pristine, hermetically sealed apartment. When the power goes out because of a storm the insects invade in a flood and Pratt locks himself in his bedroom - which is no escape.

This one is always fun as well - unless you're afraid of cockroaches, in which case you might want to skip it. E. G. Marshall plays Pratt so over the top villainous that you're pretty happy when he finally gets his comeuppance. The effect of all those bugs bursting out of his body is a pretty gross.

Epilogue

A pair of garbage men - one played by Tom Savini - find the comic from the prologue still in the trash. They look it over and discover that an ad for a 'real' voodoo doll has already had the order form sent. Back in the house Billy jabs away at the voodoo doll as his father screams in pain.

The Bottom Line

Creepshow is always a good time. It's not the best work of either King or Romero, but it's got a sense of wicked fun to it that really captures the comics it's inspired by. As with those old EC comics there's a definite sense of old-testament revenge running through the segments, with bad people getting exactly what they deserve. (Except for poor Jordy, that is.) It doesn't bear a lot of scrutiny, but it's a fun movie to watch while the ghouls and goblins queue up for some candy.

CREEPSHOW 2

"Thanks for the ride, lady!"

Director: Michael Gornick, Producer: David Ball, Written by: George A. Romero, Stephen King, Starring: Lois Chiles, George Kennedy, Dorothy Lamour, Tom Savini.

Five years after the first *Creepshow* was a surprise hit at the box office we got *Creepshow 2*, with a screenplay by George Romero based on short stories by Stephen King.

I haven't actually watched *Creepshow 2* since it was released. I didn't like it much, though I do remember croaking "thanks for the ride" to friends whenever they dropped me off. Though the segments were based on existing King stories and something I wanted to see, the general quality and tone of the film was significantly different from the original and had lost most of the 'wink wink, nudge nudge, aren't we having fun with this horrible stuff' aspect as well. It no longer felt like a labor of love - more like a budgetary decision.

The Medium
Creepshow 2 was available via Netflix streaming. The image is fine, but it's not really a movie that demands a high-def picture. In general the cinematography is just above TV movie quality - a disappointment, seeing as the director is the cinematographer from the first film.

(Arrow Films released a Blu-ray in 2016.)

The Movie
I'm breaking this out by segments again.

Framing Sequence

The animated sequence this time is a story that runs between the individual segments of the film. It follows a young boy named Billy (no relation to the kid from the first film) as he excitedly receives a new copy of the *Creepshow* comic from The Creep himself (played by Tom Savini). Over the course of the film he receives a venus flytrap in the mail (ordered through the *Creepshow* comic, natch), runs afoul of some bullies who crush his precious flytrap, kicks one of the bullies in the crotch and flees to a deserted clearing where the bullies are devoured by enormous flytraps. The animation is serviceable, if jerky, and has no real mood or atmosphere to it.

"Old Chief Woodenhead"

This is a terrible segment. It follows an elderly couple who own a general store in a dying town. They've got a wooden, cigar store type indian out front that they call Chief Woodenhead. The local Native American elder gives them a number of tribal valuables as collateral for debt the tribe owes the kindly store keepers. Later the nephew of the elder kills the couple in a botched robbery. Old Chief Woodenhead comes to life and wreaks vengeance on the killers.

This is really annoying on a number of levels, but it's also just not very good. The effects are okay, but there's more time spent waxing poetic about the bad guys' hair than in the stalking and killing. And I have no idea what to make of the whole Native American/White paternal figure/Spirt of Vengeance crap.

"The Raft"

Just FYI, in Maine such a device - a tethered, floating wooden platform for swimmers - is called a float.

Two young couples head fifty miles into the middle of nowhere to go swimming at a lake in October. Some kind of malevolent oil slick stalks them and kills them one by one.

This is actually one of my favorite King short stories (though it suffers from Inappropriate Sexy Times in both the print and film versions). This adaptation is... okay. Actually, it's not bad. It's definitely the best of the bunch. It's pretty suspenseful at times and the effects are fairly well done when the creature is attacking. At all other times it looks like a dirty floating tarp. The only likeable character is killed first, which leaves us with jackasses for most of the segment, but they all go in bad ways, so I guess that's okay.

"The Hitch-Hiker"

Wealthy adultress creams a hitch-hiker. Said hitch-hiker then keeps appearing as she goes to greater and greater lengths to rid herself of him. Each time he appears (more and more damaged from her attempts to dislodge/kill him) he mutters "Thanks. Thanks for the ride, lady."

This one is okay too. Not great, not good, but okay. The gore effects are well done and the only humor in the three segments is found in this one, particularly with the repetition of "Thanks for the ride, lady."

The Bottom Line

There's no heart in *Creepshow 2*. While the first one had fun with the concept - lighting and framing and even the general tone of the segments - this one is simply a straightforward horror anthology dressed up with some animation. And it's not even a particularly good anthology. I'd suggest watching "The Raft" and skipping the rest.

FRIGHTMARE (1974 – AKA COVER UP)

"They said she was well again!"

Director: Pete Walker, Producers: Pete Walker, Tony Tenser, Written by: Pete Walker, David McGillivray, Starring: Rupert Davies, Sheila Keith, Deborah Fairfax, Paul Greenwood, Kim Butcher.

I had this film recommended to me a few years back. I have a movie also called *Frightmare* that my brother Scott gave to me as a gag gift. It looks terrible and I've never even opened the shrink-wrap on it. (It's also known as *Paranoid*.) There's yet another film called *Frightmare* from 1983 (aka *Horror Star*) that also looks to be pretty terrible. I haven't seen it, though I remember thinking the poster looked like that of a kickass heavy metal band (it has everything you want in such a thing - skulls, snakes, knives and zombies).

Luckily, I also have a copy of the ORIGINAL *Frightmare* from 1974. This one is written and directed by Pete Walker, who also did *House of Whipcord* and *House of the Long Shadows*. I'm happy to report that this is a significantly better film than either of subsequent versions appear to be. (Though, to be fair, I'm only going on reviews and trailers for those films.)

The Medium

I recently found a copy of the 2000 Euroshock Collection DVD for $2.97 at Bull Moose. It's a bare-bones affair with nothing on the disk but the film itself. The picture quality is so-so, with many scenes appearing either washed out or too dark to make out details.

Kino Lorber released a Blu-ray version in March of (2014) and it looks significantly better (at least from the stills) and also includes a commentary track, featurette and interview. If you can find the Blu-ray, that looks like the way to go.

This also looks to be available via streaming on Amazon (free with Prime).

The Movie

In 1957 a court commits Edmund and Dorothy Yates to a mental hospital for a series of horrific crimes. Eighteen years later they're released, and Edmund's daughter from a previous marriage - Jackie - checks in on them from time to time. Unfortunately, she begins to suspect that her mom may be having a relapse...

Meanwhile, Jackie's half-sister Debbie is behaving badly. She's out at all hours of the night, egging her boyfriend into fights over imagined or invented slights and screaming epithets at her sister. Jackie's new boyfriend, Graham, tries to intervene and help Debbie deal with her abandonment and parental issues, but Debbie knows a lot more than she lets on, and she may be very much her mother's girl.

Wow. So, low budget to the extreme. Very 1970's. Pacing is a bit weird and plot twists are telegraphed a mile away. And yet... there's a lot more depth than I expected here. There's commentary on family dynamics, particularly in blended families, and poor Jackie finds out just what it's like to be the stepdaughter sometimes. There's an indictment of modern psychiatry and the very idea that anyone with a mental illness can be 'cured.' It's a crap stance, but an interesting one to explore in a horror context. There's the idea that love can be an enabling force, a weakness that allows evil to grow.

And then there's Dorothy. Sheila Keith is just amazing as the mother with an 'appetite' issue. She's at turns violent, kind, wheedling, sneaky, open, fearful, manipulative and maternal. Sometimes all of these in one scene. She brings a depth and gravitas to the role without making Dorothy the least bit sympathetic. In one particular scene she uses a feigned weakness to turn Jackie's father against her, and the look of sly, cunning glee on her face is genuinely disturbing.

Because Dorothy has indeed relapsed. And as she's a psychotic cannibal, that's very problematic. She's placing ads in newspapers advertising tarot readings for the lonely and depressed. She's got tarot cards, a unique ability to read the very lonely, and a power drill. And she's going to use them all (plus a red hot fireplace poker).

Debbie, meanwhile, has started to show signs of the very same tendency. Soon the police are involved and Jackie and Graham race to try and help her. Unfortunately for them, Debbie already HAS help.

Cinematography is hard to judge, given the quality of the DVD, but it seems as though some thought has been given to lighting, anyway. Jackie's apartment (and that of her friends) is bright, white and clear. Dorothy and Edmund's farmhouse is dark and lit with firelight most of the time, and it seems to get darker as the film progresses. Acting is above average, with Sheila Keith being a standout, of course, and Rupert Davies bringing his traditional low-key gravitas. Deborah Fairfax and Kim Butcher, as Jackie and Debbie respectively, are not quite at their level - and Butcher in particular has a tendency to yell instead of emote - but they're both charismatic and attractive. Paul Greenwood as Graham is a little too understated, but works well enough as the 'good guy.'

The general presentation is that of an early 70's exploitation film, but the skill of the filmmakers and the performances elevate things slightly.

The Bottom Line

I genuinely enjoyed *Frightmare*. It's a bit threadbare in spots, but the performances - particularly of Sheila Keith, who I just cannot praise enough - are quite good, the writing is above average for a horror film, and the ratio of plot/action/gore is good enough to keep things moving at a decent clip. It's not quite a masterpiece, but it's a surprisingly good exploitation film.

DAY OF THE DEAD (1985)

"That's right, Bub! Say hello to your Aunt Alicia!"

Director: George A. Romero, Producer: Richard P. Rubinstein, Written by: PGeorge A. Romero, Starring: Lori Cardille, Terry Alexander, Joe Pilato, Richard Liberty, Jarlath Conroy, Sherman Howard.

I have a confession to make: for the longest time *this* was my favorite Romero zombie movie. It was the first of his films I saw, which probably has something to do with it -though I'd definitely seen bits of *Night* and *Dawn*, probably through *Fangoria*. It came out when I was still in high school and video rentals were just getting going. The one movie theater in town had closed, not that they would have shown an unrated movie to begin with. While *Evil Dead* was the very first movie I rented, I think *Day* was in the very next batch of tapes.

I don't think it being the first was the only reason, though, as it remained my favorite of the bunch for a decade or more - long after I'd see the others. There was the gore, of course. The effects remain some of the most well-done of any horror movie, from 'Dr. Tongue' through the exposed brain to Rhode's disembowelment. Tom Savini is at his peak in *Day* and you can see his influence in every zombie productions since. (Particularly in *The Walking Dead* - special effects supervisor/co-executive producer Greg Nicotero's first film was *Day of the Dead*, where he worked on both special effects and in front of the camera as Private Johnson.) There was also the dark, introspective, almost nihilistic tone - particularly attractive to me as a depressive, introspective, and nihilistic teenager.

But if I'm honest there's really only one reason why *Day* held the top spot in my affections for so long - and that reason is Bub.

The 80's had a lot of what I call 'character monsters.' In the 30's you had Dracula, Frankenstein's monster, the Wolfman, Mummy, and others - protagonists as well as antagonists. In the 80's there was Jason and Michael and Freddy. Monsters that had their own agency and fan followings. And there was Bub - a zombie, yes, but also a fully realized character who is also arguably one of the heroes of the movie. Out of all the 80's movie monsters, he was my favorite.

As I got older my tastes widened somewhat (though they remain relatively shallow), and *Day* has fallen out of favor. *Night* is now my favorite of the Romero films, followed by *Dawn*. I still love Bub, though. Even as I type this I've got the Amok Time Bub figure staring at me, his reward bucket at his side.

The Medium

I've got the two disk DVD (DiviMax) Anchor Bay release of *Day of the Dead* from 2003. It was an excellent release for the time, with a ton of extras, including two commentary tracks, hundreds of stills, a documentary and even a PDF of the 'first draft' script. It still looks very good for a DVD, but if you're thinking about picking the film up in HD, the new Scream Factory release seems to be the way to go, if only for the new feature length documentary. (It also includes the commentary tracks from the Anchor Bay release.)

The Movie

A woman wakes in a white, cinderblock room. On the far wall is a calendar with the month of October showing. All the days have been crossed off. It's October 31, Halloween. She approaches and holds her hand out to touch the picture, an idyllic presentation of a family in a sunny pumpkin patch. Suddenly numerous rotting hands burst through the wall to grasp at her. And she wakes again. This time she's in a helicopter flying low over what appears to be an abandoned coastal city. But appearances can be deceiving...

In some ways this is my favorite section of the movie. The opening bit with the white room/zombie hands is cool and startling, but it's the all-too brief exploration of the abandoned city that really sticks in my head. All those empty streets, the abandoned vehicles, the debris, the alligator. I think this was really the first time the aftermath of a zombie apocalypse was presented - so many films before and since are occupied more with the apocalypse itself, rather than the results (though I'm sure there are exceptions). *The Walking Dead* has been great at following up on this, though, and the early episode scenes with Rick in the remains of Atlanta remind me of this sequence in *Day*.

Of course the city isn't really abandoned - it just doesn't belong to the living any more. The new occupants respond to the sounds of people shouting over a megaphone and the dead spill out into the streets, looking for fresh meat. Amongst these zombies is one of the greatest zombie effects on film - the so-called 'Dr. Tongue' zombie, who has apparently had his face blown away by a shotgun blast, his lower jaw almost gone, his tongue flicking about in the breeze. (I ran an *All Flesh Must be Eaten* game that included a jawless zombie - one character was gummed and the others almost shot him, thinking he'd been bit.)

Faced with the obvious - that there are no survivors in the city, or at least none that can respond - the helicopter leaves and returns to the military instillation that is their base of operations. It's an underground complex set in a old mine, a place where a ton of things - including boats and old government documents - are stored. This is where the movie settles down into its real story, about a military that wants control, scientists who want to understand, and two guys who want to just enjoy the last dying embers of a world that's already burnt to a crisp.

On the military side we have Captain Rhodes, a high strung commander with only the most tenuous hold on his men and his sanity. His second in command is Steel, a blowhard and a bully. A number of other soldiers round out the unit, including the barely-holding-it-together Miguel.

For the scientists we have the extremely tough and capable Sarah (the woman we met earlier) and Fisher (played by John Amplas, who was also the title character in Romero's *Martin*). I'm... not sure what it is they do, exactly. Supposedly they're looking for whatever caused the outbreak of undead. The lead scientist is a man named Logan, though all the soldiers call him Frankenstein. I know what Logan does - he experiments on zombies. Sometimes he carves them up - there's a memorable scene in his lab that includes a brainstem still attached to a body and a zombie that literally spills its guts - and sometimes he trains them.

The third group is in some ways the most interesting, but is also the least active in the plot. John, the pilot, and Bill McDermott, the radio operator. They're outsiders both figuratively and literally - they even live outside the underground complex, instead setting up a homey trailer deep within the mine itself. While the other groups struggle to find meaning and reason in a world gone mad both John and Bill are just trying to get by, doing their jobs but nothing more.

Most of the film is about the conflict between the soldiers and the scientists. Rhodes wants answers - really what he wants is a solution to the problem they have, which is that the dead are coming back to life and civilization has gone down the toilet. The scientists are struggling with more basic questions - like HOW the dead are coming back to life and WHY. That is, except for Logan, who really is trying to figure out a solution. Unfortunately his research requires a steady stream of 'subjects' from a corral of zombies the military keeps in the mine, and that leads to the inevitable collapse of structure and the deaths of (almost) everyone involved.

I actually skipped a group, and it's an egregious error on my part. The zombies themselves form a distinct fourth group, represented by the one zombie that Logan has managed to train: Bub. The other zombies do what zombies do, mill about aimlessly until a living brain ambles by and then they get real focused. Bub has regained some contact with what he used to be before he died. He tries to shave with a razor, read a book - he even listens to Beethoven with an expression of surprise and, maybe, joy on his face. Bub, in some ways, represents a hope for the future- the possibility of human experience living on beyond death.

All the other characters don't seem to represent anything but hopelessness, really. The military just want to shoot their way out of everything, a physical and military solution that has no chance of succeeding. But the scientists are just as deluded - they're looking for an answer where there may be none, assuming that answering a hypothetical WHY is more noble and useful than just trying to get on with HOW. And John and Bill are really the worst - though their point of view seems to be the one Romero favors. And that point of view seems to be "we fucked everything up and even if we didn't God hates us so let's just give up." The sum total of human civilization, achievement and history should be dumped and forgotten. Yeah, there's a lot of absolute crap saved away in deep places as if it should mean something, but there's a lot of good as well. Baby. Bathwater. Whatever man, let's just get high and have babies that we never teach about anything. (And how offensive is John as a character, looking back at it - a lazy, weed-smoking black man from Jamaica?)

Man, there's just something about this movie that provokes me to ramble on about nothing. I guess because that's what most of the movie seems to be about, rambling about nothing. Luckily we get a lot of gory zombie-related goodness in between the shouty bits and an extended zombie assault on the base that provides some of the only comedy available in the film. Bub is awesome and Sherman Howard just kills with his performance - bringing more life and humanity to a zombie than most of the other human characters provide.

The Bottom Line

On one level *Day of the Dead* is a depressing shitstorm of violence, nihilism, pseudo-philosophical bullshit and indictments of both the military and science. On another it's a thoughtful, introspective look at what humanity means and what, if anything, is worth saving about it. And on yet another level it's a gory zombie romp with a fantastic zombie character and fantastic effects sequences.

I feel like I've been overly hard on *Day* while writing this, and the truth is it's only in the dissection of the film that I get annoyed with it. As a whole, I still very much enjoy the film - and Bub forever, man. Bub forever.

THE EXORCIST

"The Power of Christ compels you!"

Director: William Friedkin, Producer: William Peter Blatty, Written by: William Peter Blatty, Starring: Ellen Burstyn, Max von Sydow, Lee J. Cobb, Kitty Winn, Jack MacGowran, Jason Miller, Linda Blair.

Last night we had 58 trick-or-treaters - not bad, but it felt slower than even last year, when it rained on Halloween. We've had as many as 87 and we prepared for more, given that it was (relatively) warm, dry, and on a Friday. Looks like I'll be eating Kit-Kats and Peanut Butter Cups for a few months.

We watched *Dracula* and *House of Wax* as the boys and ghouls came and went. *House of Wax* is our Halloween tradition and *Dracula* was just for fun - it's a good horror movie to have in the background as little kids arrive. When Halloween falls on a weekend we just run horror movies all day, but it was a workday and a busy one, so those were the only films we got to watch before settling down at 8:45 to watch the final horror flick for *31 Days*.

The Exorcist, not unlike *Halloween*, was one of those movies I didn't really appreciate the first time I saw it. My video diet at the time was mostly slasher films, monster movies, and anything with gore/nudity. Into that steady stream of stabbings, decapitations, boobs, and dismemberment *The Exorcist* dropped like a lead weight. I was bored out of my mind and spent a significant amount of time trying to freeze-frame the 'face' that appears during Father Karras' dream.

Part of the problem was that the primary shock pieces in the film - the head turning around, the pea-soup vomit - had already become entrenched in popular culture. I'd seen those things copied and parodied a dozen times before I got to see the actual film. To me they were elements to be made fun of rather than be shocked by.

I'd also rejected religion and embraced science in my teens. The ultimate message of the film seemed (and seems) to be that science fails in the face of true evil and religion holds the only succor. To quote my teen self, "screw that shit." Of course science had become my religion, but I wasn't going to figure that out for a while yet.

The 1990's were, for me, a time when I re-assessed a lot of things - choices, interests, life-goals, family. I went back to school, got married, and generally moved out of the mental adolescence that seemed to mark my late teens/early twenties. I got a little (only a little) more self-aware about my own biases and ignorance. (Yes, this self-referential rambling is going somewhere.) The 90's were also a decade that offered little in the way of new films for a horror fan, so in the wake of my self-assessment I also started looking at films I'd discarded or dismissed earlier in my life. *Halloween* was one of those, *The Exorcist* was another.

Halloween was honestly more of a revelation to me than *The Exorcist*. I thought I knew *Halloween* and watching it again in the 90's was like watching a completely different film. *The Exorcist* remained the film that I remembered - but *I* had changed, and my enjoyment of the movie changed accordingly. I could now appreciate the anti-science/pro-religion message without feeling like I was being attacked. I enjoyed the pace and slow buildup of fear and tension now that I had developed (some) patience. And I could shake off the cultural baggage attached to the set pieces and enjoy them in the context of the film, rather than that of society in general. And I could see how different the film was than any other horror film being made at the time. How terrifying it must have been to see for people like my mother, who had been raised Catholic (and knew the rap of a nun's ruler on her knuckles). How good it was.

The Medium

We watched the film on streaming from Amazon. I'd planned on picking up the recent anniversary Blu-ray, but it's still too expensive for me. I picked the *Extended Director's Cut* version, which has several additional scenes not found in the original release. To be honest, I didn't really like the additions and think they significantly impact the pacing, as well as confusing the narrative in some spots. The ONLY addition I like is the bit with Merrin and Karras talking on the stairs after the first exorcism session. All the new 'creepy face flash' bits are particularly annoying.

The Movie

The Exorcist opens on an archeological dig in northern Iraq - Father Mirren (the ever-awesome Max von Sydow) unearths a small statue of a demon (and an amulet). Troubled, he returns to the dig later and climbs to a high point where he faces a large statue of the same demon as the wind howls in off the desert. Though subsequent films in the series indicate that this statue is that of the demon Pazuzu and is the very same demon he defeated in an earlier exorcism, very little in this film directly references that. (Though this opening scene and a scene where Merrin's name is mentioned by the demon possessing Regan are indicators in that direction.)

Then we're whisked off to Georgetown, where actress Chris McNeil is filming a new movie. She's staying in Georgetown with her young daughter, Regan. Chris starts hearing noises in the attic, which she assumes are rats, though her butler insists there are no rats in the building. After an incident with a ouija board in which Regan refers to a spirit she sometimes talks to that she calls 'Captain Howdy' Regan begins to develop strange behavioral issues. She confronts an astronaut at her mother's party, telling him "you're going to die up there" before urinating on the carpet. She has violent outbursts and swears like a sailor. After an incident in which Regan's bed begins to bounce around like a carnival ride Chris takes her to a doctor. This begins a long set of medical tests as the specialists try and figure out what's wrong with her.

The medical tests are some of the most horrifying parts of the film. Watching the doctors basically flail around in the dark while looking for a rational explanation really set me off in the 80's, but I've since had more experience with doctors. Things are no longer quite as bad as they are in this film - the incredibly painful and intrusive tests shown in the film have been replaced by much less problematic ones nowadays - but the insistence on more tests in pursuit of theories and hunches is something I've seen a few times. I'm sympathetic - I know medical science requires a fair amount of testing and exploration - but it's just incredibly difficult to watch a loved one get poked and prodded over and over again as your faith in the professionals' ability to figure it out drains away.

Watching it this time around I was struck by the thought - what if this happened to a middle-class family? A poor family? Chris is wealthy - I mean she's got a maid, a butler and a live-in assistant. She can afford all these expensive tests and treatments. For a poor family this would be impossible. Regan would be committed faster than you can say 'ward of the state.' On top of that, calling in a Catholic priest would carry completely different baggage nowadays. In the 70's it was all about the loss of faith - Chris has no religious background and even Father Karras is having a crisis following the death of his beloved mother. Now it's less about faith and more about trust - a different kind of faith, I guess. Would you let two male Catholic priests be alone in a room with your pre-teen daughter? Though the new Pope seems to be making some progress in restoring, er, faith, in the institution, there's been significant damage done to the Catholic 'brand' over the last few decades. Trust is a lot harder to come by.

Medical science fails Chris, as does psychiatry. She eventually turns to religion and father Karras, who is both a psychiatrist AND a priest. Though suffering from his own crisis of faith he eventually becomes convinced that Regan really IS possessed. (I'm always astonished by how much crazy crap this actually takes - I'd be on the phone with the Vatican after the first time the bed shakes on its own.) The Church approves an exorcism and sends Father Merrin, the elderly priest from the opening sequence. Together, he and Karras try and rid Regan of the horrific presence that has possessed her.

Things really get cranking once Karras is on the case. Friedkin has invested a lot of time and effort into presenting a detached, clinical look at how things are building up. There's almost a documentary feel to some of the scenes - particularly the medical tests - that gives a sense of realism to the events. So once he steps on the gas and shoves us into that freezing room we're unprepared for how crazy it gets. He's established a sense of trust - yes, this is bad, but it's a distant thing - and then Regan is projectile vomiting pea soup, and cranking her head 180 degrees, and floating three feet over her bed. We've been slowly ascending a rollercoaster and now we plummet over the other side.

The exorcism scenes are top notch horror filmmaking. They're tense and awful and frenetic and terrifying. The only criticism I really have of the film during this time is the death of Father Merrin. That he dies off-screen feels like a bit of a cheat, though there parallels for Father Karras with the death of his mother, that he also was not present for. Those are not really followed up on, however, so it really just feels anticlimactic - a missed moment for me. It deflates Karras' ultimate sacrifice a bit, though that's still an effective scene.

Friedkin is a skilled filmmaker in cinematography, pacing, and direction. One new thing I noticed this time around is in the scene where the detective, Kinderman, questions Chris about the death of the movie director, Dennings. As he questions her more about Regan the camera moves in slowly, getting closer and closer. Once he abandons that line of questioning and moves on the camera starts pulling away - a neat little 'warmer, warmer... colder, colder' moment I hadn't noticed before.

The acting is generally very good, with Jason Miller as Karras, Linda Blair as Regan and, of course, Max von Sydow as Merrin being standouts. Ellen Burstyn is fine and sometimes quite good, but she reaches hysteria too easily at times and leaves herself with nowhere to go. Supporting characters are fine, with Lee J. Cobb as Lt. Kinderman being notable, though his character is perhaps a little too Columbo-cute for the circumstances.

The Bottom Line

The Exorcist is still a horror classic and the defining horror movie of the 1970's. Its success revealed and whetted an un-tapped appetite for horror among the general public and paved the way for a horror renaissance. It's a damn good film - but I'll stick with the theatrical release from now on.

MOVIE LIST

The Blair Witch Project
Shivers (aka *They Came From Within*)
The Fly (1958)
Oculus
Sasquatch, the Legend of Bigfoot (1976)
The Legend of Bigfoot (1977)
The Tunnel
Lifeforce
Zombie (aka *Zombi 2*, aka *Zombie Flesh Eaters*)
The Stuff
Big Ass Spider
The Mummy (1932)
Lake Placid
Rogue
Thirteen Ghosts (2001)
C.H.U.D.
The Uninvited (1944)
Scanners
Evil Dead (2013)
Night of the Lepus
Day of the Animals
Deep Rising
[REC]
The Visitor
The Last Man on Earth
The Last Winter
A Cat in the Brain (aka *Nightmare Concert*)
Four Flies on Grey Velvet
Creepshow
Creepshow 2
Frightmare (1974, aka *Cover Up*)
Day of the Dead (1985)
The Exorcist

BIBLIOGRAPHY

Bojarski, Richard and Beals, Kenneth. *The Films of Boris Karloff.* Secaucus: The Citadel Press, 1974.

Dendle, Peter. *The Zombie Movie Encyclopedia*. North Carolina: McFarland & Company, Inc., Publishers, 2001.

Everson, William K. *Classics of the Horror Film* (Carol Publishing Edition). Secaucus: The Citadel Press, 1974, 1995.

Kay, Glenn. *Zombie Movies: The Ultimate Guide*. Chicago: Chicago Review Press, Incorporated, 2008.

King, Stephen. *Danse Macabre*. New York: Everest House, 1981.

Muir, John Kenneth. *Horror Films of the 1970s*. North Carolina: McFarland & Company, Inc., Publishers, 2002.

Muir, John Kenneth. *Horror Films of the 1980s*. North Carolina: McFarland & Company, Inc., Publishers, 2007.

Muir, John Kenneth. *Horror Films of the 1990s*. North Carolina: McFarland & Company, Inc., Publishers, 2011.

Newman, Kim (Ed.). *The BFI Companion to Horror.* London: Cassel and The British Film Institute, 1996.

Newman, Kim. *Nightmare Movies: Horror on Screen Since the 1960's* (revised and updated). London: Bloomsbury Publishing, 2011.

Russell, Jamie. *Book of the Dead: The Complete History of Zombie Cinema*. Godalming: FAB Press, 2005.

Thrower, Stephen. *Nightmare USA: The Untold Story of the Exploitation Independents*. Godalming: FAB Press, 2007.

Thrower, Stephen. *Beyond Terror: The Films of Lucio Fulci* (revised and expanded). Godalming: FAB Press, 2017.

INDEX

Made in the USA
Las Vegas, NV
07 June 2021